Praise for *Ruffled by Grace*

Michelle Wahila weaves a path of healing for clergy and other caregiving women who have experienced toxic church culture with exquisite liturgy alongside powerful personal testimony. A much-needed resource for those recovering from the harmful side of servant-leadership.

> — Lynn M. Horan, Author, *Dismantled: Abusive Church Culture and the Clergy Women Who Leave*

Ruffled by Grace is a beautifully authentic exploration of faith, resilience, and healing that invites readers to embrace the messiness of life with courage and grace. With its poetic prayers, raw vulnerability, and rich storytelling, this book weaves together the complexities of pastoral ministry, motherhood, and personal transformation in a way that feels both deeply personal and universally relatable. It is a treasure for anyone who has wrestled with questions of faith, identity or the meaning of a calling. While critiquing the rigidity and performative nature of religious institutions through the concept of "Executive Jesus," Rev. Wahila manages to maintain a deep love for faith and community. It offers a hopeful vision of a more inclusive and grace-filled faith. For anyone seeking spiritual renewal or a reminder of the sacred in everyday life, *Ruffled by Grace* is a perfect companion for the journey.

> — Rev. Rebecca J. Craig, Author, *Once Upon a Nightmare: Through the Looking Glass of Narcissistic Abuse*

In *Ruffled by Grace,* Michelle Wahila vividly describes the particulars of her world: the passing of seasons in Paris and across the landscape of her faith. Readers are invited to look behind the curtain, to see what may be all too familiar -- burnout and grief, doubt and frustration. Part memoir and part prayerbook, this book bears witness to Wahila's dogged faith and holy creativity, as she leaves behind one dream in search of a ministry that is life-giving for her and for others.

— Rev. Bromleigh McCleneghan, pastor and author
of *Good Christian Sex: Why Chastity Isn't the Only
Answer and Other Things the Bible Says about Sex*

As someone who left the ministry only to realize I had never truly left—just stepped away from its institutional form—I deeply appreciate Michelle's honest, vulnerable, and empowering account of her journey toward spiritual and vocational fulfillment.

— David Hayward @ NakedPastor.com

In *Ruffled by Grace,* Michelle brings us on a journey through the complexities of faith, love, and church trauma. With striking honesty and vulnerability, Michelle weaves together personal stories, spiritual reflections, and liturgies that offer a space of healing and solidarity for those who may feel alone as they escape toxic environments. This book is a blessing and sanctuary for battered souls, those who have gone through the storm and emerged bloodied, but whole. This must-read will challenge the reader to a more authentic, loving, and grace-filled path through the messiness of this life.

— Natalie Drew, Author & Activist

Ruffled By Grace

Rebellious Blessings for a Fierce Faith

Michelle Wahila

Tehom Center Publishing is a 501(c)3 nonprofit publishing feminist and queer authors, with a commitment to elevate BIPOC writers. Its face and voice is Rev. Dr. Angela Yarber.

Paperback ISBN: 978-1-966655-31-2

Ebook ISBN: 978-1-966655-32-9

Contents

•

To the most Valiant Knight, the wisest Baby Chicken,
and the bravest Little Dragon.

You have loved me more than more, and you have loved this book into existence. Thank you for loving me, even when I am most unlovable, and believing in me when I can't seem to believe in myself. Because of you, my heart is ever full and ever grateful.

Acknowledgments

The words in this book are but a slice of life. They are not the whole of my life, but they do encapsulate a moment that changed not only who I was, but who I was to become. They are words about both the challenges of facing trauma and of healing. Quite frankly, the story isn't over yet because healing continues. But this chapter is now, finally, finished. As these words launch into the world, I have so much for which I am grateful. There are so many people that added to these pages with their wisdom, counsel, editing, and love.

This book is also a work of faith. Every chapter and blessing were written, edited, read and reread as a creative journey and as a spiritual discipline. There were plenty of times when I wished to relinquish this project, but the Spirit's (ahem) gentle prodding propelled me forward. Some days, simply coming to the page was the bravest thing I accomplished. Thank you, Jesus, for holding me through this project when I wept at the keyboard. It's no small thing to be able to say, "It is finished," but *phew*, here we are, and thank God.

I am thankful to the two humans who raised me with a sense of adventure and just enough faith to follow a dream, as impossible as it might seem. Without your encouragement, Mom and Dad, I would never have thought it possible to step onto a plane and move to Paris. My only regret is losing precious time with you in person. Thank goodness for FaceTime and texts; you'll eventually learn to use Do Not Disturb mode. Moving across the ocean helped me learn that love can overcome time zones. I treasure the unconditional love you have given me and hope I can pass on even a tenth of it to my own children.

I cannot help but smile when I think of Trip and Louise and all that they shared with me and our family during our time in the 'Burgh. I learned so much about what it meant to be a pastor, to bless people, and be with people, but also how to parent amid all of that – and to do so well. They taught me that church need not be dull and that taking risks for the sake of good things is always worth it.

I will be ever grateful to you, Richard. For wise counsel, for never giving up on this project, even when I wished to do so, for sharing your own story, for making me laugh, keeping me honest, and for calling me on the phone when I got quiet – thank you. There aren't really words that will adequately reflect my gratefulness so I will simply offer what I have said on numerous occasions, "Richard, I appreciate you."

Nutmegs, you made me get up at the crack of dawn to run through the streets of Paris. I was cranky and caffeinated, but those runs saved me, as did your friendship. With Nutmegs came the addition of Slow Worm, and much wisdom, laughter, and gracious editing services. I am thankful for such fierce ladies, oddities of nature, kvetching, cute puppy photos, memes and WhatsApp groups.

I have far too many words of thanks for Anna; luckily, her keen knack for editing can cure this problem. Without you, dearest Anna, this would not be a book. It would have reposed serenely in a junky computer file and have never seen the light of day. You were the first to receive the news of the highs and lows in the publishing process, and you dealt with my breakdowns like the queen that you are. You were a constant through torrents. Your care for this project and my heart were unparalleled and you poked me (gently) enough times to finish. You are everything I want to be when I grow up.

Natalie, every week you offered me a hot bowl of soup that could hide my sniffles under the guise of Thai spices. That weekly bowl of noodles was a respite, and your friendship was so much more. You were unwavering, prayerful and wise, and I needed all those things more than you will ever know. Being part of your life has been one of the biggest blessings of mine. Sharing our deepest fears, hardest moments, and every prayer request, sometimes over margaritas, is a path a friendship I would never have found without you.

Billy, you did not realize that you were getting a colleague who you were going to have to rescue, but rescue you did. You saved me from hopping my kids to school on a broken foot and probably from myself. You held hope for me when I had none. This was a most precious gift, for which I am deeply indebted.

Elizabeth, who knew that we would find our way back into each other's lives long after that Christian Education class? Your encouragement held me together during Covid. I am so glad we weren't in the same time zone and could keep each other company when the other could not sleep. So much changed for both of us, and it was not what either of us expected. Your gentle spirit and kindness are everything. I am a better pastor and a better person because of you.

To Joleen, Paige, Ellie, Allison, Pat, Camilla, Carol, Kent, Fab, Robyn, Nat, Phyllis, Johanna, Deb, Lynne, the rest of my extended family, so many friends, my writing group, countless pastors, and colleagues: thanks for listening to me talk about this book for longer than you would have liked, for reading early drafts, and for humoring me, especially when things went awry. Your insights, musings, and support helped breathe life into these pages.

With a full heart, I celebrate what you have all helped this project to become, and most sincerely, who you have helped me to become.

Spic-N-Span Friday

FIVE-THIRTY. NO. FIVE-FORTY-EIGHT. MY ALARM HAD BEEN GOING OFF FOR fifteen minutes. It was Friday. My spouse was long gone on his commute by now. I didn't even hear him get out of bed, but we had made it to another Friday. I chanted a sparkly sounding mantra convincing myself to reach for the alarm.

As soon as the buzzing was silenced, I turned to the more crucial business: email. It had been less than five hours since I checked it. I was sure I had missed something. My sleepy eyes widened when my inbox opened. The dinging of each incoming message was far worse than the alarm buzzing.

There were two from The Boss. One was timestamped after the hallowed evening meetings, and the other was timestamped with numbers that equaled "before sunrise." They were always the same format. There was something cutesy to sound relatable, followed by something I had not done. They closed with a duplicitous "grace and peace," or something equally annoying like, "In Christ."

The Jesus-y ones were the worst. I am going to tell you just how bad you are at your job "in the name of Jesus." It has more punch that way. You aren't just failing the institution; you are failing Jesus.

It wasn't even six in the morning, and I had already failed Jesus – even on my day off.

I had to get out of bed. There was no time for email. Babies needed to be up, fed, and off to school. Jesus mail would have to wait until at least eight forty-five in the morning. By then, there would be another email asking me why I hadn't responded to the previous one. There are so many ways to disappoint Jesus.

Fridays were spic-n-span day. It was supposed to be the day when I put together my house after the chaos of the week. Toddlers aren't known for their tidiness, but neither are two exhausted adults. I survived each week with a mountain of laundry and a sink full of dishes.

I had a dishwasher, but it was held together with duct tape and didn't close properly. I had to babysit it, watching it more closely than the toddlers. It wasn't worth the extra energy. It also wasn't worth asking the church to repair it: that's how the duct tape came to be.

I had a dryer too. That was *très chic* in Paris. If you had a dryer, you were *chou-chou* rich. It meant your apartment had adequate space for both a washer and a dryer. Space meant money. After all, I did live in one hundred and fifty square meters, in the seventh arrondissement of Paris.

I reminded myself of my privilege. In my head I repeated the narrative that I was so frequently told. "You're lucky to be here." It applied to the apartment and the job. "It's a privilege," I whispered to myself. I was living the dream. If only broken dreams could be held together with duct tape.

The dryer worked, sort of. The door was held closed with a magnet that wasn't manufactured by Whirlpool. For this I was glad the church sexton was so creative in his handiwork.

The wonky magnet held the door shut just enough to function, but not tightly enough to avoid the sound of an airliner taking off in my bathroom. The jiggly door aircraft could only be run during the day when there were no napping babies and when I was supposed to be four floors down in my office.

But not on Fridays. On Fridays I could run my vibrating dryer all day. It was never enough to make a dent in the laundry mountain. Then again, dirty laundry never really goes away.

Laundry first. It took the longest – three plus hours for a load. Paris washers like to live the slow life too. Then came dishes, bathrooms, and mopping. Maybe not mopping. The grocery shopping had to happen too, but in multiple rounds. If I got all the groceries my family of four needed, my Paris-sized grocery caddy was filled to the brim... and too heavy for me to pull.

Multiple market trips took me past the green and white mermaid coffee shop more than once on Fridays. I longed to stop and pay homage to my American roots, but there was no time for frivolous things. After the grocery trips there was more mail from Jesus.

Ding, ding! Dang it. I knew I made Jesus wait too long. What would Jesus do? When you do not answer with both speed and grace, you receive a meeting request. But it was Friday.

I wasn't about to give up spic-n-span Friday for a meeting request, even with Jesus himself. The same way you probably shouldn't turn down Jesus, you can't turn down a meeting request from The Boss. I worked for The Boss, sure, but there was no way that I was leaving the apartment again.

As much as my stomach turned at the thought of having The Boss in my space, I was not going to give him the pleasure of taking me out of my apartment on a Friday. He could come to me. I could serve coffee. It wasn't the green and white mermaid's sacred brew, but it would have to do.

The doorbell rang, startling me. I startled more easily now. I was jumpy and anxious all the time. "Relax," I could hear my husband's words resonating in my jumbled headspace. He always whispered when I was jumpy.

This is relaxed now – relaxed with a side of anxiety.

I shoved my uneasy contemplations back down into my churning gut and forced a smile as I opened the door, "Welcome."

He seated himself in the living room, on one of two vintage Ikea chairs. I wondered how many times he had been in this church-owned apartment.

I extended a mug filled with frothy goodness to him. It felt too kind. He must have thought so too because he dropped a compliment.

"The apartment looks great."

"Yes, I spent all morning cleaning it. It is how I spend every Friday morning."

"You don't have a cleaner?"

"I do; it's me."

I don't remember what he really wanted out of that critical last-minute meeting. Maybe he wanted to know how I spent Fridays. I know my boundaries irritated people enough to make them seek a way to investigate. Maybe he yelled at me. Maybe I blocked it.

I blocked a lot of things. It was easier that way, but I wanted to remember Fridays. They grounded me. I was real on Friday. The laundry, dishes, and groceries jumbled my apartment, but reminded me that I existed. I needed a cleaner existence that didn't beg to be blocked out of my consciousness.

Once he left, I eyed the pesky jumbo wall-clock realizing my Friday was ticking away. It was almost time to retrieve my babies from the French *maternelle* preschool. I hadn't even showered yet. I usually showered after the second grocery run, to wash off the Paris grime.

I had to wash off a lot of grime. That was the true sacred gift of Friday. On that day, I could stand in the holy of holies of the shower, and cry.

No one can hear you bawl in the shower. Like the temple curtain protected the ark of the covenant, the shower curtain safeguarded my fragile existence. Once you step into the consecrated space, what happens there is a mystery to those on the outside. I was a devout pilgrim of the tiled sanctuary on Fridays.

Holy tears flowed; the kind that were a mix of deep grief with a touch of rage. They were camouflaged by the running water and would have been undetectable if it hadn't been for my full body sobs. My body shook and tears fell. I no longer remembered the muck of all the ways I disappointed Jesus. Friday was spic-n-span again.

Michelle Wahila

A Liturgy for Shower Sobbing

The Spirit hovered over the waters of creation.
Sustenance for all beings.

Cleansing.
Caressing.
Creating.

Droplets spill gently,
Swirling my emotions.
Steam envelopes me.
Warmth embraces.

I am invited into my own tumbling cascade.
Sustenance for my being.

Cleansing.
Caressing.
Creating.

Within this tiled womb,
Secrets are held,
Grief is released,
Shame undone.

Sniffles become sobs.
Tears become torrents.
Blubbering. Breaking. Bawling.
Sustenance is found here.

Water flows and tears stream.
Whimpering and wet,
Fresh water cascades down my body,
But salt water purifies my soul.

Cleansing.
Caressing.
Creating.

What has been held inside
Bubbles, ripples, trickles forth
Until silence washes over me.
Sustenance for this moment.

The Valiant Knight of Kleenex
and the Crumpled Kingdom

CRUMPLED ON THE FLOOR OF THE CHURCH APARTMENT, THE DRAB PLACE that was my house but not a home, tears streamed down my face; my body was shaking. I screamed a series of rapid-fire questions between expletives in my husband's general direction, "Why am I doing this?"

I thought I knew. I thought I knew why we had uprooted our family, sold all our earthly belongings and flown across the ocean, but now I hesitated. I wasn't sure.

My heart felt as if it was shattering into ten thousand icy cold pieces. Numbness had taken over, infiltrating my thoughts, and paralyzing my soul. My husband reached for my hand, but I shrank away, feeling alone, tired, and broken.

It's not possible to cry any more tears, I thought. Yet, there I was, covered in saltwater, weeping. There wasn't a tissue in sight, so my sleeve would suffice.

"Do you want this Kleenex?" my Valiant Knight asked.

"No, I don't need it."

"Really?"

"No. I don't need it."

"Ok," he mumbled. "Why don't you just quit?"

"I can't quit. I am not a quitter."

"Fine."

"Fine."

I lifted my eyes, but not enough to make eye contact with my Valiant Knight. Instead, I looked around the church apartment only to see all the things that didn't belong to me. I was surrounded by one hundred and fifty square meters (1600 square feet) that were not at all ours.

At that moment, I wanted nothing more than to give into my spouse's suggestion to quit this life that didn't feel like mine anymore. Balled up, lamenting that generic church apartment, I became more resolute. I wanted to walk out of the church doors and never look back.

At the same time, though, I wanted to give my finest. The over-achiever in me wouldn't have it any other way. I had already worked myself into that crumpled up, knee-hugging little ball, and I would continue to do so. I kept going under the guise of giving my best.

I knew that I would break all the Sabbathy-rest rules I had learned in seminary. I would scoff at every self-care principle of ministry to keep going. There was a time when this "giving my best at all costs" principle would have been false. That now seemed another lifetime ago, far away from the sad, powder blue apartment walls that now boxed in my life.

I have always wanted to give my all to serve. In the before time, however, I had healthier boundaries that would have prevented me from going down the dark path of martyrdom for the job, even if it was a "call" from God. The longer I remained in *that* place, where I felt I wasn't enough, the more I would break the sacred self-care rules to achieve.

It was the complete antithesis of grace. I suffered in my perfect-ministry mentality, but not nearly as much as my family suffered. The more I hunkered down to give my everything at the office, the less my family received.

I was lured by the culture of the institution into thinking that my best wasn't sufficient. This plunged me into the pit of despair. I was spread so thinly that no one was getting my finest. I felt entirely inadequate and was completely burnt out.

To be sure, my kids weren't receiving the cream of the crop. I would come home from work to see them off to bed one or two special days a week. It was ample time to kiss their precious foreheads and remind them that they had a mother. Surely those sweet kisses were plenty.

My spouse wasn't receiving the greatest me either. He got the leftovers, after everyone and everything else was done. He received the messy, tissue-rejecting lump on the floor. I shrunk away from our marriage knowing that I wasn't achieving anything in that realm either.

Day in and day out, everyone was demanding more of me than I could give. I had laid down the enormity of my job at Jesus' feet at least a year earlier (a year into the dream job). Doing so hadn't decreased the workload: my growing guilt over not completing my heaps of tasks had just increased. The demands accumulated and I stretched out my arms further, trying to hold everything together.

I had plenty of "well-meaning" lay church leaders from various roles in the business world offering me advice. They gave tips and tricks that I was implored by The Boss to utilize in my daily routine. I may have worked for The Boss, but I hoped and prayed that the business-suit- wearing-Jesus they peddled would be proud.

Unfortunately for my institutional tasks and pinstripe-wearing Jesus, anytime I managed to feel like I was getting ahead on that paperwork, some real-life people would show up in my office.

With every knock on my office door, I imagined Jesus beside me. In my head, I saw a well-kept Jesus with dark glasses. Seated at the end of the long oblong table, surrounded by heaps of theological works on the shelves behind him, this Jesus was a VIP. In his CEO role, he looked down upon me and surveyed the situation in my office.

There was an iPad and a briefcase beside him. He was ever-ready to pull contracts and glossy presentations from his tobacco-colored leather briefcase. The iPhone near his briefcase was audibly buzzing even though it was switched to silent. He was awe-inspiringly important.

I named this institutional savior "Executive Jesus." He was mostly a jerk. I hated him really; yet, I invoked his name at the beginning of every meeting. I bowed my head and powered through to serve him.

When people came to my office, when things went awry with my day, I could sense Executive Jesus' presence over me, reminding me of my unproductive nature and pastoral failings. I could see the reports piling up on my "to-do list." They sat there longingly on that never likely to be completed list, and the pressure built.

I came to accept the daily chastisement of Executive Jesus for being unable to do it all. I never really expected balance in the role anyway. I wasn't naïve. I accepted the imbalance as a sacrifice.

Balance is never achieved, it's curated. When you attempt to achieve it, you will always be disappointed, or you will disappoint. Even when you're trying your darndest, there will be something or someone tugging on your heartstrings. I had three people pulling on mine.

"Mommy, are you going to be home tonight to tuck us into bed?"

"No, honey, Mommy has meetings again tonight."

"But Mom, you've had meetings every night this week."

In that season of ministry, I was only separated by two floors from my babies. It took one elevator ride of two minutes to get me home for bedtime. Executive Jesus clung tightly to me, chaining my ankles to my oversized desk so I couldn't take that elevator ride for bedtime.

Instead, I picked up my suitcase-sized tote, full of all the important things I needed for the evening and left my important people behind.

My heart cracked open and holding back tears I shut the door to my babies' room. I couldn't speak any meaningful words; I simply reminded the boys to behave. Executive Jesus applauded me in the background. I left the house before my tears could be detected by the Nanny who would have the joy of tucking my babies into bed yet again.

Executive Jesus had ahold of my head, but my heart was too shattered to belong to him. I yearned for a Savior who could hold all of me – my head and all the broken pieces of my heart. I was ready to breathe again, to scream and laugh, and cry out loud. I was ready to leave it all behind. I wanted to trade Executive Jesus for the life-bringing Jesus I thought I once knew.

I was ready for life and for an abundant life; one that now seemed distant and elusive. I was prepared to go from holding my breath to practicing a different way that (I hoped) would take my breath away. I imagined a new existence. One in which there would be less arguing about who is in and who is out and far fewer unread reports. There would be more love marked by eternal significance and less time spent inside the four walls of my office.

I would be able to breathe in love and exude joy. I was done with the politics, patriarchy, and parameters that held me back. I was finished with Executive Jesus who kept me from claiming the voice within me that was the very breath of God.

More than anything I longed to have a place and ached to find a home for myself and for everyone like me who felt betrayed and outcast by the institution. If this home did not exist, then I wanted to help build it.

I was just one person. I was not likely going to change the world. I wouldn't be able to change the institution of the church, but I deeply desired to embody a way forward in which the church didn't have to be merely the institution. If I needed to leave behind my pastoral calling to do that, then so be it.

I began to imagine what it would be like to create something new. What would a community of love and light really look like? What would happen if I were brave enough to talk about the scars I had? I wondered if I was ready to claim those scars so that their witness to the past could begin to bring more breath and life into my being, present and future.

I surmised that it would look almost nothing like the institution I knew. I loved the *ecclesia*, but she had hurt me deeply. I realized just how many people had similar scars and who weren't being served by the institution I thought I knew so well.

As ideas of community swirled in my head, I imagined what authentic life together would look like. Though I wasn't sure it could ever actually exist, I dreamed of what it could be.

And it wouldn't be boring. I hated dull. The monotony of my current nine to midnight reminded me of that. The Kin-dom was not supposed to be lackluster. It was supposed to be innovative and cutting edge, serving all the way to the edges where the misfits, dreamers and the forgotten gathered. Every seat at the table would be filled, the edges blurred, and the boundaries removed. We would celebrate because we were all there. Maybe we could all be a little ruffled by grace.

As much as I had come to hate Executive Jesus, I didn't want to bash the church universal. Bashing alone does not bring progress nor growth of faith. A dream of what church could be would flit around my head, and my defiance would waver. I would convince myself that the church I knew was "ok." That at the very least, it should be enough for me. After all, the institution had birthed me.

It's uncomfortable to critique a place you have called home for so many years. It's especially challenging when you aren't simply pointing out that you don't like the colors that the walls have been painted, but the very walls themselves. Nevertheless, the assessment that I began to voice came from a place of hope – hope for something better.

The evaluation was also mirrored in a wider reality – there is plenty that is broken about the church. In recent years, we have seen tremendous scandals unfold and celebrity preachers fall from glory. We've witnessed waves of people leave the darkness, hypocrisy, and exclusion of the institution behind, choosing to be "nothings" over "Christians."

For a time, I wondered if that would be my own fate. I tried my hardest to leave the institution of church behind and not look back.

The reality is that my heart was pulled toward the institution that I sort of despised. When I returned through the church doors, it was not as shepherd but as sheep, with a broken heart and little hope.

I came back with a heart cracked open just enough for something different, hoping I could leave the church building behind, while protecting and maintaining faith. My return started with the small things – simply wanting to reflect a more loving, less judgmental faith in the world every single day. I desired to work through the difficulties of the intersections of faith and everyday living.

As a wife, I looked to how my husband and I could be a couple who reflected faith, even if the institution hadn't cared for us as a couple. As a mother, I hoped to provide my children with the tools to think critically about a place that had taken their mother away from them for so many bedtimes. I yearned for a larger perspective of the church and especially of the world, a world I believe I am placed in to do good.

It seemed surreal that I could leave behind the institution for something better. I wasn't sure I could create a calling that would allow me to curate a more balanced life. It equally seemed somewhat hypocritical because I believed I should work inside of the institution for the change I was convinced should happen. I never thought leaving would be the answer to finding a more prophetic voice and a greater calling, and yet, it was.

It took time to recreate my narrative. Instead of being a rogue pastor, I was one who had found my voice, and maybe (gasp) an even truer calling along the way. I dabbled in rebellious love rather than church politics.

Some days, when I am feeling particularly salty (in the Biblical sense, of course), I still want to smash the patriarchy, tear down the institutional walls, and punch Executive Jesus. When I see young women being burned by antiquated policies designed to elevate men, when I see queer voices being silenced, and I read unclear institutional stances inviting people in but not welcoming them, I can feel the grief bubble back up inside of me.

There are also times when I wish my love had been more courageous, for the sake of my own spirit and for my family, not to mention those being cast aside in Jesus' name. There's still work to be done; I pray I can do my part. It took walking outside the church doors to have enough freedom to find love-soaked courage and a new beginning.

Stepping out into the world was the scariest and perhaps the most faithful thing I have ever done.

A Daily Prayer

Holy Spirit,
Drench me in love-soaked courage.
Amen.

The First Sermon

I wasn't supposed to be here, getting a new church job in Paris. I was just a small-town gal from upstate New York, serving the Lord in Pittsburgh, PA. I had already settled in the big city!

Besides, I was content and certainly not job hunting. I had a perfectly good church job, a supportive husband, a feisty toddler, a brand-new infant, and a place to call home. I felt rather complete in my 30-something working-mom-pastor status.

I was serving on the board of an academic institution, where one of my fellow board members told me that he had the perfect job for me. I was skeptical, because although I loved parish ministry, I was heading toward academia.

I had carefully curated my application and already met with the department chair, who agreed to serve as an academic advisor for my Ph.D. I was going to be able to pull from my experiences serving another non-profit board working in Haiti, my love for theological discourse, and desire to study liberation theology. I was ready to open a door to academia, even if it meant closing one to parish ministry.

Yet, I applied for the job. It was my fearless and faithful church elder who convinced me I should. She was a trailblazer in her own right, and she knew how to play with the big boys. With her constant encouragement and ferocity of spirit nudging me along, I put pen to paper and began to contemplate what it might be like to see myself in a new pastoral role 3886 miles away from Pittsburgh.

When I began to interview for *the* job, what quickly became known to my family and closest confidants as a dream job, I was crystal clear about two things with the interview committee: 1. I was a conscientious hard worker who would give my energy, intelligence, imagination and love to my role 2. My little family of four would always come first (My Valiant Knight, Baby Chicken, and Little Dragon).

After the committee sifted, sorted, and interviewed, in what was a lengthy process of over nine months, I was the last woman standing. After almost a year of waiting, I was flying to the City of Light to preach my "candidating sermon." This procedural event was the gold seal on it all. I was landing my dream job. The congregation was, in church-speak, "calling" me, a country girl from rural New York, as the next associate pastor of their sizeable and thoroughly dynamic, international congregation.

I twiddled my thumbs as the plane readied for take-off. The flight attendants were taking their last run through the cabin, slamming shut the overhead bins, but I was lost in my own ponderings and the chaos around me was like a white noise machine lulling me deeper into contemplation. I pursued this. I followed each sign dropped from heaven so closely and now here it was, upon me.

The final task of the nine-month interview process and following "the plan" was a single sermon delivered in worship. We were wheels-up as I began to go over my exegetical notes and manuscript again for the three thousandth time. I pressed each page of my paper notebook between my fingers as if I was trying to embody the words themselves. I had preached a thousand messages before this one. It was just like any other sermon. At least that was what I kept telling myself.

Eight hours and a restless jetlagged sleep later, it was soon Sunday morning, and the concluding assignment was rapidly approaching. From plane to pulpit, I hotfooted it toward the Neogothic stone archways that beckoned me inside to complete the task at hand. The time had come to step into the pulpit of the church that would soon become my congregation and my new place of residence.

Climbing the creaking staircase that led to the raised stage-like pulpit, ornately carved with famous Reformation figures, my knees were trembling beneath me. I gently tiptoed up the stairs to the top, being careful not to clap down my stiletto heels and make too much noise. As I reached the second to last stair, I glanced at the candles flickering on the altar, watching their tiny flames dance without inhibition. The breeze making the flames sway was cool, but I was warm and slightly tingly in my extremities. Who was I to be here, in this pulpit?

With my exquisite black peep-toes, I searched for the edge of the final stair that led to the pulpit platform and reached for the light. I flipped on the light switch and imagined the Holy Spirit to be illuminating the words I was about to speak. "Please, Great Comforter," I prayed silently to myself. "Speak more loudly than me." I'm not sure if it was fervor or nervousness driving the prayer, but it didn't matter because the time had come.

My knees never stopped quivering, but my heels were firmly placed onto the aerobic step which had been situated in the pulpit just for me, so that I could see over its greatness. I stared out at those gathered to listen. For decades people had gathered in that place to hear some good news, to sense the Spirit's prodding in spoken truths, and to learn more about living in community.

Today was my turn to deliver.

Before I was able to open my mouth to speak, I mentally ticked off the A-list of incredible preachers who had stood in that pulpit before me. I sucked in the deepest breath I could find before words began tumbling out of lips marked by the sacred hot pink gloss that was my "preaching lipstick," "Come, Holy Spirit...." Still wobbly, I felt as if my voice was quivering, and cracking, but maybe not. I wasn't sure.

I wondered if my voice would stand up next to those who had come before me. Faithful installed pastors, famous preachers, and social justice warriors brought the Word faithfully in that place over the ages. As my exercise in contemplating my smallness concluded, I wasn't sure any words were going to come out of my mouth when I opened it again.

The responsibility of preaching was real, it always was. Today, though, the pastoral stole I wore around my neck was extra weighty. In worship, the scarf-like yoke hung around my nape over my academic robe since the day it was placed there at my ordination.

A symbol of servanthood, this pastoral accessory matched the colors of the liturgical season adorning the church sanctuary. My vestments complimented the embellished hanging banners and the cloth that covered the dark wooden communion table in front of me. The ornately embroidered stole with tiny green metallic threads, signifying "ordinary" liturgical time, defied how very extraordinary the moment was (at least for me). I stepped into *that* pulpit in *that* place – overwhelmed with apprehensive joy.

For three services, I knocked my knees together, and I spoke. I was whisked in and out of worship by a committee member assigned to shepherd me and keep well-meaning congregation members at bay. Past the grand stone columns, I glanced at the opalescent Tiffany windows glimmering in the light as I was rushed through the grand oak door on the side exit of the sanctuary.

My physical movement in and out of worship was furiously rapid. We moved so swiftly that I began to feel that time was synchronously speeding up and slowing down. "You're almost finished, and then you'll be able to rest," my shepherd whispered, with a properly comforting pastoral tone. Those words of solace would become my battle cry, but not this day. On this Sunday, in *that* pulpit, in *that* place, I was welcomed with an *aperitif* after worship.

The anticipation of "what was next" was electric, and I was thrilled to be in a space with so much potential. Along with dozens of church leaders, I raised my glass of lightly golden Chablis and toasted to the future. We laughed with heads tilted back and chattered about the things and people and places that had come before. Primarily, we dreamed out loud, contemplating together the innumerable possibilities of what God was going to do.

Little Dragon slept peacefully, unaware that he was in the middle of cocktail hour. My sweet baby was tiny enough that he was still nursing every few hours and, therefore, my weekend travel companion. I positioned him perfectly on my left hip and we wove ourselves in and out of those gathered. Dressed in his old man plaid suit with a bowtie and newsboy cap, he was (as my mother would say), "Cute as Christmas." He was irresistible to everyone, being passed around from person to person, cheeks duly squeezed. With every pinch of his cheek, I imagined this welcome reflected what our new church family was going to be like.

My Little Dragon was going to grow up in a family where the depth and breadth of humanity was represented. He was going to be comfortable among this woven tapestry of peoples – Grandparents, Aunts, Uncles, Cousins, Siblings. He would come to know this community as his family when we departed our blood family on the other side of the ocean.

That Sunday was filled with copious amounts of "things": preaching, nursing, smiling, greeting people, preaching, nursing, preaching, small talk, *aperitif*, and smiling. Toward the end of all the things, I wasn't sure what time it was. Between jet lag, adrenaline, and the abundant amount of spring light to which I was unaccustomed, it didn't matter what time my dainty bracelet watch read. The rays of sunlight invited me to press on, and I willingly obliged, pushing self-care into the Seine.

After the goodbyes were spoken, I closed the imposing brown wooden church door behind me to return to my boutique hotel situated neatly on the corner of a boulevard whose Haussmann buildings stood tall, glimmering in the shining rays of springtime dusk. I could feel the exhaustion, but my full heart was the only thing occupying my mental space.

My enthusiasm was so intense that though fatigued, I couldn't sleep. I pulled the hefty, stripped blackout curtains hoping I could entice myself into slumber. Propped against a silky crimson pillow, I sat in the darkness of my teensy hotel room for one, gazing upon my Little Dragon, wondering about the details of life so far from our family and friends in Pittsburgh. We had built a home of welcome, perfectly joy-filled with laughter and love. Surely, I thought, the same kind of home awaited us in Paris.

Michelle Wahila

A Prayer for Firsts

For firsts that delight and dazzle us,
We revel in riotous joy.
For firsts that terrify us and make us tremble,
We bask in rabble-rousing possibility.
For the ways in which You hold us,
Through every first,
Until the very last,
We relish
The unruly grace
Of this promise.

Picture of a Move

THE MOVING TRUCK ROLLED AWAY WITH THE VERY FEW CARDBOARD BOXES that contained the entirety of our remaining "things," including a few keepsakes and a few extra baby onsies. The golden sun was setting on the final day in our cherished home. My photographer friend showed up to snap one last family photo in front of our beloved Pittsburgh townhouse. It was going to be a feat of heroinism to capture it – we were all close to a "moving to a foreign country" meltdown.

In the forefront of all the glorious meltdowns known to humankind was my overtired toddler, Baby Chicken. His fluffy chick-like strawberry blonde hair bounced back and forth as he bolted like lightning around the edges of the yard. The only thing grander than his cowlick was his personality. He zoomed toward the camera and cackled like a TV personality vying for his close-up. My dear friend had her work cut out for her.

As she attempted to wrangle Baby Chicken, I held my bobble-headed number two. Little Dragon was squarely on my left hip. It was as it always was. Though the house stood practically empty now, nothing seemed to have changed. Nothing was different, and yet everything was being refashioned.

We had lived for almost a decade in that "starter home," and had renovated it from top to bottom. We had pulled off musty petal pink and mint green wallpaper and unearthed ancient brick fireplaces, and in doing so had created a place for Christmas stockings to hang. We became masters of tile cutting and drywall. Measuring twice before cutting, sometimes we still failed miserably in our DIY renovations.

With fuzzy rollers and big brushes, we painted every square inch of that place, more than once. We rolled periwinkle blue and bicycle yellow onto the walls. We had imagined selling our cute lil' first home for a larger one with a great big yard. Instead, we were trading our equity for a small but already furnished apartment in the center of a city we did not know.

The swishing pampas grass in the back corner of our front yard caught my attention. It's gentle rustling whispered words of hope for what was yet to come. Transported from my nostalgia back into a moment of pure chaos, the gentle photographer was rather unsuccessfully attempting to arrange us on our recently painted front steps. "Everyone, look this way!"

Worn out from packing moving boxes in between nursing sessions, I gazed not at the photographer, but at our home's crowning jewel. The garden was our home's oasis. What was once a barely-there grassy mud patch surrounded by a chain-link fence was now a lush flower garden. Vegetables stood at attention tucked in between the flora. It was only right that our final family portrait would be taken in front of our garden on Jackson Street.

I marveled at the remnants of our urban sanctuary growing around the "For Sale" sign in the front yard. I remembered the way that the day lilies danced in the late spring breeze, pictured the rare burgundy lily sprouting up from the edge of our green space. I had planted it in memory of my grandmother. With every stir of the flowers, we inhaled the delightful scent of the mint that was standing summer-tall near the empty spot where the tomatoes should have been planted.

Our ever-patient documentarian adjusted and readjusted our slightly agitated, wiggly bodies. We sat on the front steps long enough for her to snap a couple of photos. Eventually it was a successful picture of flip flops and no makeup, cargo shorts and raggedy white t-shirts, fatigue and anticipation. The "realness" of the photos captured the sacredness of our Jackson Street home – everything that it had become to us over the years.

The pampas grass rustled again, and I lifted my gaze heavenward. Cotton candy shaped puffy clouds dotted the summer sky. Perfect picnic sunshine warmed my face the way joy warms you from the inside out. Little Dragon started to grunt discontentedly. His delicate peachy little fingers squirmed, and his pinky rouge lips began puckering like a guppy. "Momma's got you. Let's eat, Little Dragon."

We had shoved everything we thought "essential" into two suitcases before we watched the moving truck haul away the rest. The "rest" was the few possessions we chose to ship to our new "furnished" residence, mostly baby items that would be needed immediately. It was months before we would see our belongings again (so much for "immediately"), but it didn't matter because we were following the "Divine plan" laid out before us. We had what we needed, and we had each other.

We landed in Paris on a balmy and brilliant late-summer afternoon. We emerged from the transport sent to fetch us from the airport with an almost holy anticipation. Holding hands, our eyes fixated on the Eiffel Tower that was our neighborhood's designated touristic landmark. Today she wasn't a daydream. She was real, set against a cloud-free backdrop that appeared so perfect it looked photoshopped.

It was the kind of Parisian day that when you face heavenward, you can only see the cerulean sky. Late August never disappoints with those uninterrupted blue-sky days. It leads you directly into the cooler September but still graciously clear days, which convince you that Paris is, undoubtedly, the most beautiful city in the world.

In the loveliest city, I had procured my dream job and thus it began. For what seemed an eternity, we lived out of two navy blue suitcases. There was no time for romantic sentiment, or to settle into a family routine or to unpack properly. The work began the instant I stepped into the magnificent stone building that was both my place of work and my new home.

Michelle Wahila

I was welcomed into my new pastoral role by eager committees that hadn't met regularly for months, volunteers that were burnt out long before I arrived, and a host of new administrative tasks that over-filled most of my days. I missed my very first staff meeting because I was torn between singing outdated Bible songs with children and the Business Manager who had me on speed dial. I was signing my name a mere ten thousand times on mounds of French bureaucratic papers required to live in Paris when my jet-lagged brain remembered I was supposed to be elsewhere.

The jet-lag ultimately wore off, but the fog of a new existence did not. I stumbled back home at the end of each lengthy workday via the silvery metal elevator conveniently situated in my place of work. Each day I glanced in the mirror on the back of the elevator wall. The sagging dark circles under my eyes only heightened how disheveled I looked. I would muse to myself, "I am a workhorse in this workhouse."

Every day, I stood in the metal tin can of an elevator inside the fish-bowl that was my place of work. Time passed and the bright autumn skies turned to the grey and somber skies of Paris in the winter. It was a well-paced descent into disappointment. I saw my existence fade away. In the same way, I saw the shadowy circles under my eyes grow darker. I wondered if the people watching the fishbowl could see it too.

—————

A few months of elevator rides later, I turned away from what I hoped was an evil enchanted elevator mirror and not my actual appearance and inserted my extraordinary secret key into the numbered slot that would whisk me away from work. The turn of one powerful silver key took me back to our fifth floor apartment (labeled as the fourth floor in Europe's numbering system that began with zero for the ground floor). As I staggered over the threshold, the elevator doors closed behind me in the fourth or fifth-floor hallway, wherever I was.

I could already hear the restlessness behind the once-varnished-now-partially-peeling door on the left side of the hallway. Before I could get my house key into the lock, the door cracked open, and I was greeted by one crying Little Dragon who missed his Momma (or maybe his Momma's milk) and one energetic Baby Chicken who was the king of his toddlerdom and thus annoyed by the lowly peasants who had been serving him before my arrival.

I went from one job to the next upon stepping through the entryway of the enormous wooden doorway that separated work from home. With Little Dragon already squarely on my hip and one Baby Chicken wrapped around my leg, I scooted in slightly further to also greet my Valiant Knight. He faithfully kept the castle up and running while I adjusted to my workload. His new role as Knight of the House wasn't lost on me.

Once I wrangled the sticky Baby Chicken off my leg, I glided over the slightly slippery wooden floor planks toward my big person. I reached out to greet my number one and I quickly came to nestle my forehead between my spouse's pectorals. With equal speed his arms wrapped around me, and he kissed my cheek. It was the first solace I found all day.

On the other hand, my dear spouse was raring to go. Stuck at home waiting for his mythical work visa to be delivered, he busied himself with domestic work. Copious amounts of baking and feats of gastronomy occupied him while I worked four floors below. As I rested in his embrace, I inhaled the scent of freshly baked sourdough and lasagna Bolognese.

My own productivity paled in comparison to that of my Valiant Knight. I could never get it all done. Nevertheless, I found routine. Learning the ropes of a massive institution consumed every synapse I had. I took notes at each staff meeting and would pore over them afterward in my apartment. With neon-colored sticky notes and highlighters in every color, I organized and prioritized, assuring myself that Executive Jesus would be proud. Each night I prayed that I would soak in everything on my lengthening "to-do" list by osmosis. Rising before the sun every morning, I sucked down a pot of rich dark espresso before I found myself back in the shiny silver elevator that would lower me into the belly of the institutional beast.

In the confines of my subterranean office, I twirled in my too-big-for-my-petite-frame chair, not quite ready to begin work. The early 1970s carpet offered me a whiff of wet dog. I flipped off my pink patent leather stilettos, but decided the carpet was too grungy to be a place into which I could settle my toes. I slipped my pointy-toed pumps back onto my feet and rose from my work throne. I reached for the window to jimmy it open.

Pressing my forehead against the glass, I surveyed the outside through the antique leaded rectangles. I stood motionless, attempting to gaze upward, and wondering where the sunshine had gone. Not finding any sunbeams, I shrugged and slid back into my oversized black faux leather office chair as I flipped on my ancient computer tower. I fumbled around, trying then failing to enter my password on the foreign French keyboard that I pecked at like a pigeon searching for breadcrumbs in the park.

With every passing morning elevator ride, my dungeon office grew darker, not just because my sunshine disappeared but because my workload was ever-increasing. Unfinished tasks darkened my positivity, but that was inconsequential. I pressed onward. With each mission of the establishment that I completed, there were twenty more awaiting my attention.

I was behind from day one, which I suppose was to be expected. The great stained-glass institution had plenty of monumental tasks with which I could occupy myself. I watched the papers on the corner of my desk become a pile of unsorted assignments. It multiplied daily even as I compelled it with a stern biblical prayer to "Shrink behind me, Satan!"

My sunshiny optimism over moving to a foreign country became clouded just about the time that cerulean Paris broke up with me, leaving behind the murky nothingness of grey sadness. The azure early autumn sky of Paris leads to the sooty sky of late autumn Paris. Late autumn Paris inevitably leads to the darker drab atmosphere of Paris in wintertime. I am not sure what months this period covers. We call it, "the grey time", and it lasts approximately one thousand two hundred and forty days from January until April, or May, depending on the year. While my running list of things to do seemed to squeeze me, time slipped through my fingers.

Like many days, I wasn't sure where the day had gone. It had been full, and a blur. I locked the door behind me to take the longest two-minute elevator ride ever to the apartment. Though I now always tried to avoid it, I caught a glimpse of myself in the vile back-of-the-elevator-mirror. Like most days, I was certain that I looked worse than the day before. My complexion matched the clouded atmosphere of Paris. I turned away from the looking glass, jumped slightly at the elevator's ding and emerged on the other side of those metal doors setting my gaze homeward.

Michelle Wahila

A Moving Prayer

Though doubts and disappointments hold me back, push me
forward.
When I am tempted to stand still, give movement to my feet.
If I begin to waver in uncertainty, anchor me in faithfulness.
Lend discernment where I lack trust, and encouragement where
there is fear.
Each time my heart is pulled toward the past, thrust me into the
future with enough hope for the present.
Let me live this day with love, knowing that I am but a
sojourner here.

A Cuppa Home

THE HONEYMOON PHASE OF MY INTERNATIONAL WORK ROMANCE WORE OFF more quickly than I imagined possible. Like I would after any good breakup, I sipped a goblet-sized pour of *Côte du Rhône* wine for dinner and cried myself to sleep. The daylight hours and my wine-sipping-time were shorter now.

Time both stretched and condensed to simultaneously make my workdays longer and the time I was supposed to be resting my head on a pillow shorter. Days and nights were full of much of the same – task after task followed by the fear of not being able to get it all done. Sometime between the moment when the lapis blue Paris skies turned exceptionally grey, and my late autumn workload peaked, I missed "home."

I scrolled through all the places I had lived previously in my mind. I wasn't sure where home was. Pittsburgh, or NY maybe? It certainly wasn't Paris.

Autumn is a particularly fantastic time in the Northeast United States. France did not provide all the glorious fall handiwork of God in quite the same way. The transition from summer to fall in France is always rather abrupt. One day there are ultramarine skies and sunshine and the next there are simply low-lying stratus clouds that seem to usher in perpetual dusk.

Once we begin to see the somber dark skies dominating, we know it is time to hunker down for the next several months, because we won't see the outside again until we are picnicking on the Champ de Mars with our *baguettes* and *rosé*. The allure of springtime in Paris may be romantic, but it is a perfectly scripted Hollywood lie. Paris is pink blossoms, sunshine, and love for approximately three seconds a year. The rest of the time it is cold, dark, rainy, and above all, grey.

The bleakness of the Northeast winter was always tempered by the incredibly vibrant colors of the King Maples, Northern Red Oaks, and Sycamores that surrounded me in the upstate New York version of autumn. Throw in some bright orange pumpkins and ruby red candy apples, and the drab cloudiness was much more tolerable.

I adored fall in the Northeast. I soaked in all the sights, sounds, and smells she had to offer me each year. The musty scent of hayrides, and the saccharine salty mix of corn popping in a caldron-sized kettle were staples. I watched bicyclists plummet down muddy hills and jump over boulders in cyclocross races while sipping the refreshing crisp flavor of freshly pressed Concord apple cider. It gave me life. Every sight and smell of autumn would instantly take me back to my child-hood, even as I had my own family and created a new narrative with a husband and two wee ones. If a season could be "home," fall would always be welcoming me with open arms and spicy cinnamon.

Walking the streets of "autumn Paris" was none of what I knew the fall season to be. There were no pumpkins, no hayrides, no candied apples, no bike races and no kettle corn. There were no sunny cool days where you could stand outside in tattered-in-all-the-right-places faded jeans and a puffy down vest admiring the merlot-colored maples with a thermos of hot mulled cider.

In Paris, I would rise reluctantly each fall morning, only after hoisting my white flag at the battle of the snooze button. I searched my enormous but mostly vacant bedroom closet to find the warmest and coziest number of layers in my wardrobe. The tank, the extra tank, the light and flowing long-sleeved shirt, covered finally by the equally billowing wool cardigan and the *écharpe* – always, forever the *écharpe*. With these many layers and my scarf, the penultimate French accessory (surpassed only by the ultimate accessory of the red lip), I prepared my body to exit my apartment and brave the Paris mist.

The mist is the cruelest of Paris weather because it's not enough precipitation to warrant an umbrella, but certainly enough to ruin my hair, makeup, and mood. Was it rain? Fog? Pollution? Or a mix of some European precipitation of which I was previously unaware? The moist miniature blobs had a way of attaching themselves to everything, enveloping me in a dampness that matched the reluctance of my spirit. I may have been walking in what people told me was the most beautiful city on earth, but I was covered in tiny droplets of Paris mist about as far from home as I could be.

Armed with my fashionable scarf, I couldn't work harder to assimilate to life in France. I may not have been given the opportunity (or time off) for language lessons, but I did what I could to "fit in." I had to do some shopping – mist or no mist.

I hadn't taken a proper lunch hour that week, or ever, (a sacrilege in France) and my family all needed a few odds and ends because our things were still on a ship somewhere in the Atlantic. Mostly I was tired of seeing the same monkey onesie on my youngest that appeared to mock me with its catchy phrase, "I'm bananas for you." Everything felt bananas.

Our family tried to dress the part and do French "things." My Valiant Knight acquired a pair of those entirely too skinny Skittle-red pants that all the *Frenchies* were wearing with their pointy-toed Oxford shoes. I took to true Crayola red lipstick and a completely black-on-black wardrobe. I had "taken" to French espresso, sipped with the proper amount of poise and attitude at the corner café. Nevertheless, every time I walked by *that* coffee shop adorned with the green and white mermaid, I longed to stop and pay homage.

I resisted because it was everything *but* French. I could hear my dear spouse's sarcastic remarks in my head calling me out for my "Americanness." I walked by *that* shop every few days to drop off and pick up the littles from school and *halte garderie* nursery care, which gave me an excuse to both be outside and work on my little French persona.

I turned my nose up at all those people inside with their mocha-frappe-fru-frus. I resisted my pilgrimage to honor St. Arbucks in the most pious way. I tossed my silky French scarf around my neck and sauntered by, not tempted by the aroma of roasted beans more powerful than any incense wafting through the doors of a French cathedral.

I puffed up my chest and arrogantly glided by, congratulating myself for my superior assimilation skills and ability to resist. I kept this snobbery up with glowing reviews by my very assimilated spouse until we were deeply embedded into autumn. I am sure the feast day of St. Arbucks is sometime in October on the day her most valued creation of all time is introduced each year. I saw the festival banner waving outside, and I was drawn in by the two words that made my heart full: pumpkin spice. There was no resisting it.

The glass doors slid open and welcomed me inside. The sweet smells of home filled my nostrils. The aroma was spicy and sugary like the final dessert course of a Thanksgiving meal. I allowed the mix of nutmeg and cinnamon to infiltrate – breathing the present moment in deeply and allowing childhood memories to flood my consciousness.

In my broken French I ordered the biggest size they offered. The barista had the ability to make the green and white *goblet* glide down the marble counter and directly into my grasp. The cup practically melted into my hands; my heart melted along with it. I could feel its warmth and smell its spiced goodness. I knew that the perfect combination of the bitter roasted beans and syrupy joy awaited me. It was autumn in a paper goblet. If I could have shoved everything I ever loved about home into a cup, it would have fit into that *venti* sized vessel.

I carried it back to our apartment, practically weeping. I missed home, wherever that really was. Yet, there it was in the container I was bearing. It was warm and inviting. I laughed at myself and all the ridiculousness that was me, holding this coffee, becoming overwhelmed with joy. The more I pondered its goodness, the more I thought that the feeling of holding this oversized paper takeaway receptacle was a holy feeling.

I walked back into our empty echoing fifth-floor apartment and - with the recognition that I held home in a cup - broke into tears, leaning against the all-too-happy powder blue walls that greeted me at the door of my otherwise unoccupied dwelling. With my back against that cheery wall, I slid down toward the old wooden planked floor, hoping to avoid splinters and holding my paper chalice close to my heart. I wished that takeaway goblet would infuse its goodness into my soul. There was more intimacy in that cup than in the space where I was now crumpled.

Hunched over, I stared at the mostly vacant space adorned with country kitsch by which even my grandmother would have felt knick-knack embarrassment. I picked myself up off the partially varnished planks and settled into my vintage-Ikea snowy white couch (*such* a great choice for a family with young boys). I prayed that I wouldn't spill this precious nectar on my couch, while hopeful its goodness would spill over into my life.

Michelle Wahila

An Autumn Blessing

As the days grow shorter, remind me that darkness can bring the comfort of rest. As the leaves fall around me, give me the grace to know that life holds both moments of death and rebirth. As the cool autumn breeze blows over my face, let me rest in the knowledge that your Spirit guides through every season.

Coffee, Diet Cola, and a Dream

THERE WAS A TIME WHEN I COULD RUN ON COFFEE AND A DREAM, WITH A side of diet cola. In the pit of this Paris life, my Pittsburgh life seemed like a distant past one. It was not just home that had abandoned me but the creative vision for my life's work. I didn't know if I had given into the pressure of Executive Jesus breathing down my neck or just given up.

Life in my wet-dog-scented office was so far away from the life-sized pirate ship I helped construct for Vacation Bible School or the ten thousand pumpkins I assisted in rotating on our church lawn during the month of October when we hosted a community pumpkin patch. I sat in my cubicle and sorted through a deluge of paperwork, guarded by an army of gummy bears, and pondered on how this was nothing like my former life. I once had infinite energy fueled by joy. Now, no matter how many times I prayed at the altar of St. Arbucks, I was uninspired, unimaginative, and out of energy.

High on caffeine and stress, I resigned myself to thinking that my lack of energy was merely a side-effect of unachievable expectations. Mine was a job designed for no less than ten superhumans. This wasn't unlike any other church positions in that respect – every position is typically unachievable in some manner. It leaves room for growth – for dreams that only the Holy Spirit can fulfill. It leaves plenty of space for miracles too.

This was not miraculous. It was the opposite of miraculous, whatever that might be. Maybe it was the sacrilege of the mundane. I was under the impression that working in the church should never be ordinary. Yet somehow, without a dream, I was being swallowed by monotony. In the past, every newsletter, budget sheet, and community event was holy. It oozed the Divine, and I showed up ready to be drawn into the Spirit's movement.

In Pittsburgh, when I accepted the call to serve a church, I was presented to the committee – Presbyterians love their committees. It gave them a chance to drill me about theology and ministry and anything else in between. I skipped through the door, confident that they couldn't dissuade me from the Spirit's nudge to accept this call.

I hadn't become staff expecting to be full time. I was hired to train a volunteer and eventually phase out the paid position. As a seminary student, paid work is good work, and I accepted a part-time role. What I hadn't expected was to fall in love with the saints and work of that place.

As my affection grew, so did my role. I was approved to complete my field education there, so I didn't have to transition out of the parish. The Spirit, being who she is, summoned the winds to blow, and things began to change. I grew into a pastoral role within a congregation evolving / flourishing in love and mission.

With the addition of *moi*, we began to envision more children's programming, intergenerational ministries, different mission activities and a young adult group we affectionately referred to as YAMs (young adult ministry). I became one of the Presbyterian Women (I brought down the average age by a few decades!), led Bible study, worked the bazaar and rummage sales, learned the secret punch recipe and even learned to "lunch with the ladies." My days were full and abundant.

You can imagine my surprise then, when the committee validating my call asked why I would want to serve a smallish "dying" congregation.

"Dying? Are you kidding?" I probably sounded a bit too sassy to the committee. "My role isn't to grow programs, build new things or raise money. My job is to serve with energy, intelligence, imagination, and love. I am called to walk with people through their darkest valleys and to their highest mountain peaks, and I am called to witness to the work of the Spirit already in that place. And she is doing much…"

She was. What was supposed to be six months or a year, at most, turned into a decade of ministry and life together. I gained terrific colleagues ("terrific" was one of my boss and Gracious Mentor's favorite words) and was blessed to share my life with the saints there. Good work was done in the name of Jesus in that place.

That Jesus seemed a rather sketchy fellow because I wasn't sure he'd followed me from Pittsburgh. Now, like the air in my tiny unventilated office, life and work were stale. It wasn't just that there was "too much" on my plate. It was more than that. A long time ago, in a past life, I could walk into my Gracious Mentor's office and pitch a dream. It could have been the most off-the-wall idea on the planet, but if it was for the good of the Kin-dom, my dear mentor would give a resounding, "Yes!"

Maybe it would be a "yes" with reservation, or one that required a budget sheet and action plan, but it was always a "yes." That "yes" was his way of dreaming imaginative Kin-dom work together. It was full of give and take, push and pull, but it was a decisive "yes" that reflected the abundance of the good. He taught me to believe in good things.

It always started the same way. I knocked on his open door, "Got a minute?"

"Sure!" He whirled his office chair around toward the doorway where I was leaning against the frame. "Come on in and have a seat." The invitation to come sit across from him was always given.

Almost as quickly as he whizzed his chair around to face me, he lifted his feet onto his desk (always crossing right foot over the left), reclined to his office chair's capacity, and placed his interlaced fingers behind his head as he asked, "Whatcha got?"

In the next minute or forty-five we went back and forth with every, any (and all) ideas. There was a sense of being caught up in a holy plan so intimately that if it was fulfilling the purpose of the Kin-dom it would happen. It didn't matter how impractical or improbable it appeared.

There wasn't ever a whole bunch of "no" followed reluctantly by a "yes." For my colleague and mentor that would have been contrary to the Very Big Boss's character. God always gives a resounding "yes" to us, which he taught me should be lived out abundantly in our life and work. Every conversation with my mentor reflected the reality of that "yes" we firmly believed.

Don't misunderstand, sometimes I would waltz in with what I thought was the most remarkable idea ever, one that would likely reinvent how we all did church ministry, and my Gracious Mentor would begin with a grand pause. He would swivel his chair around toward me, but instead of propping his feet up on his desk and leaning back into his thinking posture, he would lean in toward me. Crossing his arms, he would ever so slightly glance over his spectacles in my direction and wait in silence. The silence wasn't ridicule but it was a pause. Laughter surely followed, but the bifocal stare and arm crossing happened first.

Arm crossing with an over-the-glasses glance did not equate to a "no." These were some of our best moments together. We imagined what seemed so ridiculous that it would be unachievable – those were the times when you could tangibly feel the breath of the Spirit in the room. I would get giddy with excitement as we bantered back and forth. We would cackle and argue; we would speak of the idea's impossibility, and we would decide that a Divine "yes" was worth the risk of failure.

After we crossed our T's, dotted our I's, he would release me from his office into the world, sent forth with the vision that continually drove us forward in that place. Every time I left his office I felt like some sort of prophecy was coming to pass.[1]

My Gracious Mentor's office was so far removed from the musty carpet my oversized chair swiveled over. There was no one to offer weekly banter. There was no arm crossing and no holy pause. There was no colleague on the other side of an open office door welcoming me into conversation and no one listening to imagination breathed into being. Prophecies ceased and the grief had settled in...

I couldn't touch the ground with my toes, but I wrapped my feet around the leg of my desk and pulled myself toward my computer and back into reality, whatever that meant. With my insides all twisted and heaviness in my heart, my existence left no place for dreams. That holy banter and sacred envisioning simply ceased. I had lost my ability to dream.

I was labelled all sorts of things. Doubtful, skeptical, maybe even faithless. I didn't care about those labels. The label I longed for and missed the most was "dreamer."

---

1. 1 Joel 2:28

Michelle Wahila

A Welcome to Worship

A Call to Worship written for Union Presbyterian Church, Endicott, N.Y.

Gather in, beloveds.

You are welcome:
The wanderers and wonderers,
The dreamers and disillusioned,
The brokenhearted and the brave.
There is a place for you here.
God meets us all,
Exactly where we are
Exactly as we are.

Locked In

AFTER THE GLORIOUS FEAST OF ST. ARBUCKS PASSED, I STRUGGLED WITH everything – work, family, life. I was grieving the loss of seeing my sweet babies grow up in day-to-day real time. The reality of leaving behind everything I knew in America set into my soul. Far from home, surrounded by dark grey stratus clouds, I couldn't tell if it was the weather, pollution, my dark mood, or a combination of the three, but the initial joy over the dream job was pretty much gone.

It felt sacrilegious to hate a space that was part of the church but the more I looked around the church apartment, the more I began to despise it. Too many times, I heard how "lucky" I was to have such a big apartment in such a great location. Our *arrondissement* was so *bourgeois*. True, the space was generous, larger than our townhouse in Pittsburgh. We didn't need space.

Teeny toddlers love space. They can practice moving their chubby legs at speeds far too swift for them to control their limbs. There was plenty of falling and much exploring in a brand-new space. Too much exploring for my nerves.

We moved into an adult apartment. Plenty of sharp corners, no gates, an enormous mirror that was not made of tempered glass, and a splintering church kneeler (likely some relic that someone was afraid to throw away and stashed in the Associate Pastor's Apartment) adorned the flat.

During our move the apartment was supposed to have been prepared for us. The idea of that welcome felt lovely; the coming together of the community preparing for our family's arrival made it seem like it would quickly feel like home.

It did not.

I spent my first late autumn in Paris working and chasing tiny explorers, heroically saving them from sharp corners, and following the new stashing-of-crap protocol that helped fill the church attic to excess. I said goodbye to the kneeler as quickly as I could get the splintering burden out. Not all burdens can be stashed away with such ease.

It became evident that we needed child safety locks on our windows. I thought I had requested them before our move; I must have been mistaken. We lived on the fifth floor. Open windows, high buildings, and tiny explorers don't mix.

I requested those pesky locks again. This time the Sexton ("church-ese" for building caretaker) arrived at my door. He was a genius, but his handiwork afforded the institution the opportunity not to care properly for their property (or should I say people?). Whoever happened to be making the decisions that day (decision-making remains a mystery to me even today), sent the Sexton but no locks.

He hemmed and hawed in the living room for a while. Carefully, he examined each single-paned window requiring a lock. He mumbled, "It's going to be pricey," then turned around and walked out of the apartment.

Not fifteen minutes later, he rang our doorbell. With tools in hand, he entered the flat announcing he had designed an "excellent solution" for our child lock problem. It was the speediest excellent solution I experienced in that place.

Assuming the solution was actual child locks, I stepped aside for him to work. I peeked at his accoutrements, instantly realizing he was jerry-rigging child safety locks for the fifth story windows of our Paris apartment. The ones that happened to open to one of the busiest streets in the city.

As he worked, he would stop, tinker around for parts, and subsequently resume. He made random small talk as he sifted and sorted. Sometime within the first five minutes of this rhythmic cycle, I slipped into my own thoughts, though I was nodding politely every few minutes.

"Moving is big work, isn't it?" he muttered in my direction.

"Yup, sure is." Though my agreement was a gross understatement for, "Yes, I remember that I recently sold all of my earthly goods and moved my entire family across the ocean to take this job that now will not pay for child safety locks on my windows." But "Yup," was what I sputtered out.

I stood with my hands on my hips and lips tightly pursed as I glanced over the Sexton's shoulder to read the price tag on his inventive solution. I tried to stand tall enough. I could never manage to stand tall in that place, even to protect my own babies.

Little Dragon and Baby Chicken were worth more than the six euros and thirty-nine centimes per lock, at least to me. The most "excellent solution" isn't always the right one. The "right" thing became more and more elusive to me in that place.

After collecting his tools, the Sexton bid me farewell, and I collected my thoughts. Surely, this was some sort of mistake. I glanced around the mostly empty apartment, sifting through my own crowded thoughts, replaying what had just occurred in my head.

My internal dialogue was rolling fast and furiously. "This was the one thing I requested before our move. It was the only damn thing."

———

With my Momma Bear delirium, I stepped out of my apartment to descend to the zero floor. I reluctantly pressed the elevator button. "Zero" was beginning to take on new meaning.

I waited with annoyance for my turn to enter the usually inaccessible fortress that was the grandest office. Hidden behind a dark ligneous portal, it could have been the entranceway to another realm. I imagined my own Valiant Knight near the entryway to the door, standing ready to defend our family's honor.

I went with his strength and courage because Lord knows, I didn't have my own. I was the new girl, just trying not to cause a problem. I hated being the problem.

My insides were in turmoil, but I was composed, and cucumber cool on the outside. I shrunk from Momma bear sized back into my petite self and held my breath before entering the office. If I held my breath, maybe I could gain enough oxygen to fortify my soul for the conversation that would happen on the other side of the door.

As I entered The Boss's boardroom sized office, I was greeted by the shiny oblong table that served as a reminder of opulence and an inherent imbalance of power. Your seat at the table was assigned – anywhere but the head. The stale air smelled of old books and ego.

It shouldn't have been a surprise to me that when it was finally my turn to speak, I was given the briefest of moments. He was busy and important, and I was less than. When I spoke, I trembled in front of him.

Most of my Boss-conversations had, lately, started with the phrase which now fell from my lips: "I'm so sorry. I was hoping the window safety locks would have been installed before our family arrived."

Like most of our conversations from the start to the finish of my tenure, he looked at me rather blankly and nodded. Without so much as a verbal cue that he was listening, he moved on to the next subject. I had work to do. With a single head tilt, he appeared to write off our family as "not his problem." It was without so much as one coherent or compassionate sentence.

The "problem" of two tiny explorers – one nursing and one frisky with wobbly legs – were four floors away. They weren't worth two-thirds of six euros and thirty-nine centimes. I began to wiggle more uncomfortably. He looked away, back toward his desk full of importance.

I was certain he could look through my personhood into something else weightier and darker. The longer I stood listening to his voice, the more convinced I became that I had no right to grumble about child safety locks at all. From the beginning, I started to believe the story being woven for me.

I exited with the same cucumber cool with which I entered, but now I was sure that my Momma Bear hysteria had certainly, undoubtedly, been misplaced. I was mistaken and promptly dismissed. Our family settled for jerry-rigged locks on our windows that broke the day the first gust of wind blew through our flat.

It wasn't more than two weeks after my ground-zero meeting that I pushed open the apartment door with my foot because my hands were full (my hands were always full), to see the friskiest of the tiny explorers with his tussled baby chicken hair on the window ledge. Every tiny explorer has the instincts of Houdini and bravery of Evel Knievel. Mine was no exception.

With chubby toddler fingers he had managed to open that fifth-floor window; one of the ones with no child locks. Everything in my hands tumbled to the floor. I moved with speed but without sound so as not to startle the Baby Chicken happily exploring the city from above.

I wrapped my arms around his little torso. He was unfazed by my panic and content in his exploration. I slammed the window shut, twisting it to "closed." My hubby was already by my side, and the tears were already falling.

It had only been a second that Baby Chicken was out of sight.

Seconds on the fifth-floor count. Thank God so do inaudibly hotfooting Momma Bears. At the edge of a window's ledge, I could have sat holding that Baby Chicken forever, but tiny explorers move quickly. He was already off to a new adventure. I wasn't sure I would recover from this one.

There was a gorgeous orange sunrise over Paris. It was always incredible to look out over the Seine and see the sun glistening on the water. I was living my #dreamlife, hoping against all hope that yesterday had been a nightmare. My racing heart told me that it was not.

I slid out of bed to prepare for the day. Whatever was on the agenda yesterday had become irrelevant. Today there had to be a more excellent solution to the problem of upper story windows without child locks.

There was a descent to ground zero, followed by a return to the fifth floor. I would wait for the Sexton, I was told. He arrived, eventually, with tools in hand. I breathed a sigh of relief and the sight of his electric screwdriver.

"This won't take long," he assured me. I assumed his efficiency with child locks. There was drilling and some hammering; I knew we would soon be safe.

Tapping away through the apartment, I left the Sexton to work unbothered this time. "Done!" I heard him from the back room. I left my work laptop so that I could admire his handiwork.

"Show me how to open them." Those child locks can be adult proof too.

"Oh, it doesn't open."

"The child lock doesn't open?"

"No, the window."

"Huh?"

"Don't worry. I screwed all the windows shut."

And he had.

It was an enormous space in the heart of the *bourgeois 7éme arrondissement* of Paris, with its windows screwed shut. That was our home. I was embarrassed that I didn't Momma Bear hard enough. Don't worry; we were locked in now.

A Liturgy for Fearful Moments

O Divine,
Help me stop -
To be still
And
To pause
Long enough
To breathe.

O Divine,
Help me to remember -
That my circumstance
Is
Not me
Nor the sum
Of my life.

O Divine,
Help me to move -
Toward the good
And
Toward love
Courageously enough
For one step.

Holding the Cup

SUNDAYS SERVED AS VARIETY WITHIN MY OVERBOOKED WEEK FULL OF meetings. I always rode the clanking perhaps-soon-to-break-again elevator down to my dungeon office with reserved joy for the gift of something different for the day. A ding sounded my arrival on the minus one floor. It almost sounded like church bells.

It was before eight, and one of the few times during the week that the stone building didn't reverberate with sound. It was silent – only because it had not yet come alive. I inhaled the quiet into my soul and veered toward my office.

By eight forty-five, the building was bustling. I entered the hallway and immediately could hear my name being bellowed from multiple directions. Sometimes it was simply the cry of, "Pastor!" and which-ever one of us was closest would answer. The stream of pastors coming and going from calls in *that* place made me wonder if yelling, "Pastor!" was more efficient than learning my name.

Sunday may have been the shortest workday of the week – a normal eight to four or five, but it was the most intense. It was every email, phone call, pastoral call, meeting, and text of the week crammed into a single day. In every minute that was not worship, I was surrounded by the people who made the parish come alive. With a coffee cup that miraculously filled itself all morning (by the hand of one saint), I greeted, hugged, smiled, cried, and prayed with people.

———

I snuck into my office to "robe" before worship. Jostling the black academic robe hanging above me, I slid it off the hanger into my clasp. I did an entertaining two-step dance to wiggle my microphone cable up through my non-pocketed women's clothing (those suits were not meant for women preachers). I placed the little black sound box awkwardly on my belt.

"Is this thing on?" I double-checked the mute button approximately ten thousand times before zipping my robe. No one needed to hear my embarrassing pre-worship pep talk rituals.

Post wiggle dance and pep talk I turned to my wall of stunning pastoral stoles. Red, green, purple, blue, white... Every liturgical season was set before me in the vibrance of these handcrafted beauties.

Today it was ordinary time. It wasn't Easter, Lent, or Christmas. It was just ordinary. I disliked that liturgical designation. No Sunday ever felt ordinary to me. I reached for my favorite stole; a quilted mostly spring-green stole with a perfect rendering of my former church building stitched into it.

The choice was a hot debate in my head. "I wear this one a lot," but I didn't have time to overthink. I clung to the stole for a moment, running my fingers over the stitching of the little brown church. I hung on to the memory of church I once had.

Hurrying out of my office I placed the green stole around my neck. With that yoke, my worship brain took over, and everything else became a background hum. My focus shifted to the power and purpose of Sunday. That was my work.

———

Still, I had to make it from my office to the sanctuary, and there were people in the halls and other spaces I'd have to move through. Some I looked forward to seeing. Others, not so much. "Lord, have mercy on me, I am a terrible pastor." There were plenty in the crowd who were ready to remind me. One tiny-heeled step in front of the other, I held up my robe and penguin waddled on.

There were always people who antagonized on Sundays: those who harped on the hot button issue of the day or the fusspots who critiqued every movement, outfit, hairstyle, and lipstick choice. It was like an unwritten rule in the church community – the best time to provoke is on Sunday, when the pastor simply does not have time to deal with controversy. Their voices were loud and disorienting as I tried to maintain focus on the work of worship.

Once I walked through the great wooden doors of the sanctuary and into worship, the "people I didn't want to see," faded into memory. Their voices were silent now, though I had been adeptly avoiding them three seconds before. They couldn't stir controversy when we opened our lips to speak of the Divine.

I looked out at the congregation and was overcome with what I assumed was joy. It felt like warm sunbeams on my face, but it may have been the stage lights illuminating the chancel. If I squinted, I could almost see the back of the sanctuary. The room was full.

Everyone sat patiently waiting for worship. They were illuminated by the rays of sun coming in through the stained glass that decorated the sides and back of the great stone walls. Vibrant and stunning colors danced along the slate grey: Nature creeping into the building, trying its hardest to remind me that God was everywhere – inside and outside the sanctuary.

The dancing colors were intense – enough that I immersed myself in their beauty instead of the words now being spoken from the important part of the sanctuary. I longed for peace and realized the colors were creating contentment. Imagining myself catching a glimpse of Jesus himself in the congregation, I wondered if I would recognize Him. Could he be out there, among the people?

Enveloped by the security of color and light, I rose when it was my turn to speak. Long after the interviews and my first sermon in the enormous pulpit were behind me, I still felt wobbly when I rose. Click-clack-clickity my little heels went, not up the stairs to the grandeur of the old pulpit but down the stairs toward the people and to the Table.

I reached toward the cup, firmly placing my hands around it. I was always fearful that I would spill it everywhere, being forced to watch the blood of Christ pour out around me and onto the white linens that dressed the oak table. This fear was set in the back of my mind just waiting to be realized. "Not today, Satan!" I raised the chalice with both hands decisively placed.

Every Sunday I raised the cup of salvation, and the people would come. As the congregation came forward to receive the Holy Meal, I saw a parade of saints. It was remarkable.

Over and over in repetition, but without losing a drop of meaning, I spoke holy words. There was a full spectrum of life in the eyes of those who I served. There was grief, and joy, hardship and triumph, all set within the beauty of the saints who ate the holy meal, saturated in swirling light.

Serving these beloveds of God was the greatest of privileges. As each individual came to dip their bread into the cup, they came with their own experiences of life and faith. It was not lost on me that most of those coming forward were, like me, a long way from home. This place, this moment, was home for them, just as it was for me. We were all sojourners.

The Cup was heaven's version of "takeaway home." It wasn't unlike my pumpkin spice frothed milk and espresso that had faded into my fall memories. I revisited my warm takeaway-home-in-a-paper-goblet every fall, but The Cup was a strangely reminiscent weekly version. Each time I picked it up, raising it for the congregation to see, every-thing was exactly as it should be. The warmth and excitement I felt while holding each of these cups was how home felt.

Holding my pumpkin spice latte was the perfect mix of nostalgia and an invitation home. I knew home when I saw and tasted it. Home wasn't a spicy aroma in The Cup, but it was an invitation powerful enough to gather every person in that sanctuary; it was a summons home. We were all there to taste and see the comfort of something good – something real.

One by one the people would stream through the "takeaway" line, sipping the grace of familiarity in the home found in the stone sanctuary. I held it tightly in both of my hands. I may not be the green and white mermaid, but I knew that the humans there longed for the same things I did.

In the same way I walked through the sliding glass doors of my sanctuary of St. Arbucks and was greeted by name (yes, this speaks to how often I was found there), we all long to be known, greeted and embraced. We hope for a place to belong – a place where we can come and be welcomed with open arms.

One at a time, everyone had their moment; The Cup poured out for them and an invitation to the feast of home. They need not speak any words – not even to order. The menu was always the same.

As the table closed, I asked the same question as always: "Have all been served who wish to be served?" The silence was full and holy. I meticulously placed the silver goblet back onto the table and covered it with a perfectly snow-white cloth, believing there was a *venti* dose of grace large enough for everyone.

When everything was covered in white linen again, I left the table, to return to the pastoral pew in the front of the sanctuary. Like Dorothy, I fancied clicking my heels and finding myself home, wherever that was. If the feast is movable and the saints are moving, home can be anywhere.

I was seated again, back in the big pew, glancing down toward the table. I felt that I must have taken a circuitous route back up the stairs toward the front of the church away from the saints because I was such a long way from the holy moment that had just passed. Is it possible to dream of the sacred and of home?

The organ brought us victoriously to the end of worship. I was deep in reflection and mouthing the words. I couldn't carry a tune, so I

Michelle Wahila

would never risk singing into an accidentally "hot" microphone. It wasn't without passion, just without voice; that sentiment rang ever true.

Major chords rang out into the sanctuary. Jubilantly, those around me raised their voices in praise. My mouth moved, but not a single note snuck out. I was concentrating on the colors exuberantly flowing through the stained glass anyway.

It was meant to be vibrant here. The imprint of heaven on my heart showed that to be true, every time I held the communion cup in worship. The kaleidoscope of primary colors danced on the grey walls descending downward toward the Table. My calling was vibrant too.

Maybe pastor was not the right title for me. I felt myself smiling as we collectively joined our voices (yes, even mine) in the last verse of the hymn. I left the sanctuary, marching with the other pastors that day – but not as "pastor."

I had taken a new job title for myself, "Barista of the Vibrant." I'll be the one holding two cups, one for me and one for you. We can walk together, with our takeaway coffees, on the winding path that will lead us home.

A Coffee Prayer

With the sun I rise, giving thanks for slumber and all that now resides in my past. I will start afresh. There is goodness placed before me; I hold the warmth of morning in my hands – renewed with anticipation for today. I breathe in the scent that rises from the cup; it is both bitter and sweet. I am reminded that life holds both, as I raise the cup to my lips. I will not shrink away from the bitter, nor rush through the sweet. Instead, I will consume both with love; let the whole of my existence be an offering to You. Before I taste what is before me, I pause, inviting myself into this day with intention. I will drink with gratitude for all that will come. I swirl the cup, stirring its goodness – let my heart be stirred with the same. I draw the cup closer, inviting You too. Allow me to sip the joy set before me, and savor the truth that you, O Divine, are the giver of all good things.

A Loaves and Fishes Kitchen

MY LIFE WOULD HAVE BEEN SO MUCH EASIER IF I COULD HAVE JUST STOPPED caring. That was never on the radar, however. Not caring would have gone completely against my philosophy of ministry.

It was caring that was the very heart of who I was as a pastor. I never hid that. Quite the contrary, I said it over and over and over again. I reminded anyone who would listen (and those who wouldn't) what drove me as a pastor. If I said it a million times it wouldn't have been enough to be heard, but I let the words to the church at Thessalonica ring in my ears and propel me forward into authentic ministry that cared: "Because we loved you so much, we were delighted to share with you not only the gospel of God but our lives as well."[1]

It was outside the realm of my existence not to care. In fact, caring too much would be what got me into trouble the most often. Even if I could not protect myself, I was going to protect those around me – staff and volunteers alike. Whenever it was posited that I was overreacting, I would simply respond, "Let's see how it plays out in reality."

In the end it would be me, the dedicated team who gave their all, and not a damn other person in the kitchen cleaning up until all hours.

---

1. 1 Thess. 2:8

When others took their pie in a to-go container and deserted us, we stayed. Beyond that, we stayed joyfully.

We may have been tired, but we would crank up the tunes and do whatever we needed to do. Whether it was washing dishes or rearranging the rooms, we were used to pulling a rabbit out of our hats to make things happen. I saw miracles created by the most generous, creative, and loving people.

Our kitchen team knew the miracle of loaves and fishes well. We often saw our budget line shrink, while the expectations of what we would provide grew. Maybe we didn't feed 5000 with five loaves and two fish, but some days it sure seemed that we did. Some evenings, as we cleaned up after an event, moved tables and chairs, and washed every dish from the meal, we would simply look at one another and we knew what everyone was thinking: "That was a miracle."

It was those teams who showed me glimmers of a Jesus I once knew so well, one small kitchen miracle at a time. The kitchen team was stretched thinnest, but they always came through. They were the loaves and fishes kitchen team. Their giftedness was only outweighed by their generous spirits. No matter what the unreasonable expectation of the moment was, I learned more about abundance than scarcity in the kitchen. In that place there was only abundance, not just of food (which there was), but also an abundance of time, and most importantly of heart.

In a place that seemed to function on scarcity, in the kitchen there was always abundance. We may have been standing up to eat, so that we could quickly go back to work, but it was a moment when time would stand still for me. In the kitchen, we came to a table that reflected what life together should be – filled to the brim with the nourishment of covenant-community.

Their miracles proved to me again and again that I believed in a God of abundance.

I loved living life in community, so it made sense that I enjoyed preparing for community events in the kitchen. The reasons were many, not the least of which was a truly remarkable team of faithful volunteers who made them happen. I would pop in to encourage them, and they would encourage me. I enjoyed being in the kitchen; it was really like my second office. It felt close to home, and so did the people.

On the most miraculous days when I would stop by to help work, I would be nourished not only in soul, but also in body. Whatever the team was cooking for the event would give off a heavenly scent. As I ascended the stairs to the kitchen, I could smell the homemade goodness wafting down the staircase. On those days, I would have more than gummy bears and coffee filling my belly.

When I opened the door to the kitchen, the welcome was like being greeted by family you haven't seen in a long while. Open arms, open hearts, and food-a-plenty. It was the truest sanctuary I knew in that building.

There was always food waiting with a plate placed aside for me. I don't know if they really knew how much that platter meant to me. The often-chipped dinner plate filled with warm culinary delights was a heavenly provision set aside for a hungry pastor with an empty tummy and rather empty heart.

There were real hugs, laughter, and conversation. Sometimes we had hard conversations. No matter what the team shared, it was a safe place. I did ample holy listening in that space.

I didn't want a perfect church – far from it. I wanted a transparent experience of God through the community of faith. Equally, I didn't want to simply settle for the "all of humanity is broken," and therefore the church cannot function. Yes, there is brokenness in this world, but when we move the church down to the lowest common denominator, we also remove the hope of something better.

If we see the church as only broken, we will miss miracles, if we see the community as perfect, we are kidding ourselves and setting ourselves up for disappointment. Somewhere in between the pit and perfection, there is a happy medium where we are called to live joyful, justice-seeking, abundant lives. This is where we find truth, authenticity, and genuine love.

Love is found in the everyday nitty-gritty sort of life that we share together. This is where God shows up: when we show up. We trudge together through the battles of life, big and small. We climb to the top and applaud one another, together. We learn empathy, encourage, and embrace one another in everyday things.

In all honesty, I am still learning how to live into this kind of love. We will catch glimpses of life's love stories in each other. When we laugh so hard with a friend and end up in tears, or we cry so much no number of tissues handed to us by our Valiant Knights could clean us up, that is when we spot those rare glimpses of heavenly love.

How could I choose to not care, when I saw others loving so well? I cared because the abundance of heart with which they served deserved protection, applause, and appreciation. They deserved to be loved with my whole pastoral heart and given the entirety of my pastoral energy. They deserved the pastor I was at my core, not the lame duck pastor I came to be.

I cared all the way to the finish line. I cried most of the way there too. The tears were both simple frustration and an offering of gratitude for those with me in the deep – serving, caring, cooking. Perhaps my tears were the most holy offering I gave in *that* place because they were real. They were the tears of authentic life; one lived out in a place that valued a polished final product, more than the process. Inside stone walls that tempted me to lose faith entirely, there was blessing in the abundance of life in the kitchen.

An Invocation for Abundance

God of every harvest,
Though the cruel complacency of scarcity tempts,
I will sow abundance into this life.

Let me sow plentifully into this world that which I seek to reap –

I will press into the earth
Joy
That I might reap celebration.

I will ground myself in
Kindness
That I might blossom in compassion.

I will sprinkle my days with
Care
That I might grow a tender heart.

I will plant
Authenticity
That I might cultivate love.

God of my harvest,
With joy, kindness, care, and authenticity,
I will sow abundance into this life.

The Boardroom and a *Bise*

I WASN'T UNAWARE THAT AS I GAVE MY HEART (AND ALMOST EVERY WAKING hour) to this job, another narrative was being formed. From time to time the wind would blow, and I would catch a hint of it. Simply drifting my way, the rumors whispered but were cutting.

Though I claimed my seat around the table at the monthly board meeting, I sat silently. I had few words left to speak. I knew the ones I spoke would not be heard. I crossed my legs and arms, preparing for whatever war might be sparked around the table that night. I had my iPad and my sparkly pen, along with my lady briefcase that served as a computer bag, a diaper bag, and a suitcase to create my day-to-night looks.

Even before the real meeting began, there was the pre-meeting. This was the small-talk and jockeying for position around the table. I never spoke, unless prompted. Selecting the first grey folding chair I came to that was inconspicuous, I slid into it without giving a thought to the chatter around me. If I sat perfectly still, I was certain that I could completely avoid being seen.

As people trickled into the boardroom, the *bise* began to happen. The *bise* is the French greeting – a little peck on each cheek. It was a piece of culture and power all at the same time. There were a few

81

people in that room who I just stopped greeting with that kiss. I under-stood that if you once gave someone the *bise* and then stopped, it was an insult.

I was careful and selective with my refusal to kiss. With the others I maintained the weirdness of a *bise* unwanted. It felt like the kiss of a frog you were hoping would transform but didn't. My stomach turned when they approached me. I braced myself for the physical contact that I did not want.

The meeting convened. I waited for my turn to speak, ready to present months of work on a perfectly-put-together spreadsheet. I had graphs, numbers, charts. I didn't come with my feelings – I had repressed those ages ago when it came to this job. I came with the results of an experiment. I wrote it all down. Every meeting, email, visit, call, and worship service was included.

Though earlier I pretended to be invisible to the humans filing through the door, now I felt a little less transparent. I had a special alliance with Executive Jesus that night. He was always trolling me, but especially during the night meetings. The hallowed night meetings seemed the most sacred because they seated the powerful around the table for what seemed an eternity. Tonight, Executive Jesus was going to be so damn proud of me. This time I had finally gotten it right and appealed only to logic to make my case.

Lately, the wind had been blowing around a story about my perfor-mance. I was "hyper focused on my family" and "not giving enough" to my job. I heard that I was a whiner and a complainer. People were "gob-smacked" that I would ask for so much – such as a proper day off.

I had heard similar narratives woven about other staff. I never quite understood how it happened. New employees would come. They were the most awesome ever - until they weren't. Nothing was ever good enough once they had fallen from grace. Once a misstep was taken, it was all over. There was no recovering. The campaign would begin. Your story was told behind your back and sometimes right to your face.

You are broken.

You are a problem.

You are not good enough for the job and a general drain on the staff resources.

The committee made a poor choice when they chose you.

My spreadsheet wasn't enough to undo whatever narrative had been woven. It was now the fabric of my existence in *that* place. It didn't matter if I created something new, built community, designed, implemented, or achieved. My narrative was set in stone. Not even Executive Jesus could save me.

Once I started to believe that narrative about myself, I received it on every level. It became my story as a pastor, as a wife and as a mother. It was as if I had been turned to stone myself. I couldn't move forward or backwards to fix things. It just was. It was a stone-cold existence.

I presented my spreadsheet anyway. My fate was sealed. I was not long for this role. I had already turned my focus to dismantling the system. The system should never be touched.

I was asked to leave the room. I knew how it was going to go; so, it didn't matter. I was a complainer. I made this place worse, not better. I had no more value than the ink and paper on which I had written my report. I could be used and recycled because you can always sell the dream of Paris to someone new. History spoke for itself.

After the time of discussion, I returned, practically tiptoeing back into the room. The air was a bit heavier. I noticed that it was dark. I'm not sure it had been that dark before I left. I wasn't sure how long I had been sitting outside. I felt like an outsider on the inside, well before I was asked to leave.

Not much was said. There were looks that I largely ignored. I shrunk back into my folding chair, crossing my arms. Even in my preparedness, with my pretty pie chart, Executive Jesus abandoned me that night. My report was filed "circular," and another chapter of my narrative was written. I added "liar" to the next part of my story. Even though my work was compiled into the prettiest report ever written, it could not be true – for Executive Jesus told me so.

We finally bowed our heads to end the meeting in prayer, and I gasped for air. It was the first time I had taken a full breath since coming back into the boardroom. With the "Amen," I rose quietly, said goodbye and pulled my magical "home" key from the bottom of my briefcase diaper bag, taking the longest two-minute elevator ride home.

It was late by then. Every meeting night was late. My dear spouse had given up thinking that my "It won't be super late" tagline was real. Maybe that was a lie I told myself to keep going, but it was also a lie that I parroted to him nightly.

Maybe it was not a lie as much as it was the false hope that I would see him that evening. Maybe we could share a glass of wine and a conversation about our workdays. We used to do that.

Every meeting night ended in the same way. I was exasperated and exhausted by the time I finished, even though I hadn't been afforded but a dozen authorized words that night. I took the clanking elevator ride to the fifth floor and tiptoed into the apartment so that I wouldn't wake anyone. I tiptoed often.

I silently entered the room; the same way I entered every room.

A Quietly Worded Prayer

Divine one, can you hear me? I don't want to bother you. I know I am small, and you are so grand, but maybe I can talk, and you will listen. I have run out of words that feel worthy to speak. I have lost the voice that you gave to me. So, can I practice my words with you? If you whisper back, I promise to listen too.

There will be Champagne in the Tomb

MY FEARLESS BESTIE AND I SAT IN THE *CAFÉ* CACKLING LIKE TYPICAL American tourists. I was laughing so hard there were tears streaming down my cheeks. What the heck had our waiter just brought us?

"It looks like a meatball."

"I don't think so. We are in a French restaurant. It's duck, isn't it?"

"No ducking way!"

"I ordered duck."

"But it's a ball."

"Oh my God. It's duck balls."

I hadn't been out in months, so it must have been the seclusion talking. Perhaps it was the glass of champagne I gulped down before the *entrée* arrived, but whatever it was was making me giggle, I wanted to bottle it and put it in my purse for later. I had a travel-sized communion kit. Why couldn't I have a bottle of joy inside my purse?

I imagined taking out that tiny bottle of joy from my black handbag and worshipfully receiving it. With a fervent prayer, I envisioned anointing myself with joy like the oil of gladness promised in the Psalms. If I could take the magic bottle out of my pocketbook and apply the contents to my temples like the peppermint oil that soothed my stress-induced headaches, I would have joy... so much abundant, life-giving joy. Its scent would rise like an offering, and I would know that my current situation did not determine my worth.

Through the laughter, I could feel it welling up inside me, burning through me. I chortled loudly. Was this joy? I laughed uncomfortably. Nope, it wasn't joy at all. It was anger.

It was a rare treat to be out in public, or to feel like I had a life outside the building in which I worked, lived, and worshipped. I felt it now, I was incensed. I was so ducking angry. Being in the outside world, sipping my glass of champagne and laughing with a friend, made me realize just how irate I was.

The belittling I endured during office hours paled in comparison to the outside life I lost. "I used to have friends!" I thought to myself. I used to have girls' nights, sushi nights, and dates with my husband. I used to take my kids out for ice cream, even when working ridiculous hours. I used to have joy.

I searched for the tissue I stashed in my sleeve like my grand-mother. I always had a tissue handy for those unexpected tears. They visited me frequently.

The tears I was wiping away reminded me that happiness was fleeting or eluding me. I felt so trapped in my current hell that I wasn't sure I knew what happiness was, so joy? Forget it. Was joy BBQ duck balls and *un verre*? Maybe. The laughter and bubbling anger were as close as I had come to joy in ages.

A Champagne Blessing for Everyday Life

Spirit of the Divine, You come to encourage, challenge and bless us daily. Yet, we too often reserve joy for only the biggest events of our lives. Help us to imagine that there's no scarcity of joy – that even life's little moments are worth celebrating.

We admire the golden foil seal –
Give us the courage to unseal joy.

We pick up the weighty bottle –
Offering to the universe those things that have weighed us down today.

Turning the chilled glass in our hands –
Give us the grace to feel what is before us; even when we fear we might shatter.

We hear not a pop, but a gentle champagne kiss –
Bring us insight to remember that not all significant occasions arrive with a bang.

Pouring gently into the crystal *coupe* –
Give us the wisdom to see the ways you pour abundance into our lives.

Tiny bubbles rise.
Bulles of joy
Presented to the Divine
in gratitude for the moment.
Santé!

Lazarus

I ONCE HAD A SEMINARY PROFESSOR TELL ME THAT WE HUMANS PREFER THE
hell we know to the mystery we don't. I didn't understand what he
meant back then. Perhaps I was too young, or too idealistic. Even in
my darkest night, I wasn't sure that I would say I preferred hell. It just
hadn't been dark enough.

I couldn't anticipate choosing hell, but here I was. Alone in the
darkness, I wondered how I got here and equally wondered why Jesus
hadn't shown up. Jesus had been there, done that, so we don't have
to... So much of my former evangelical upbringing resonated in my
soul incessantly reminding me that Jesus had "done it all for me." His
death rendered me free from death, but here I was stuck in the
damn pit.

Much of forming my pastoral identity was centered around
walking with people through life's transitions, pointing to the work of
the Spirit already happening in their lives. It seemed disingenuous to
point to the work of the Spirit in the lives of the people who I was
serving and not be 'strangely warmed'[1] by the Spirit's movement

---

1. John Wesley, *The Journal of John Wesley*, ed. W. Reginald Ward and Richard P. Heitzen-
rater (Nashville: Abingdon Press, 1988), 246.

myself. Choosing to stay in the pit made me feel even more inadequate. How could I possibly shepherd others when I couldn't even shepherd myself?

There were moments when I would fight back my own tears during worship. They would be increasingly difficult to suppress by the third service of the day. As I raised my heavy arms up in the air and laid my weary spirit at the cross, I wouldn't be able to fend off the tears. I would be alone in a crowd of worshippers, a sobbing mess, trying to hold it together enough to get up and do the next thing.

But the worship routine was not nearly as fatiguing as the meeting routine. Worship had life and breath and (at least some) creative moments. It was the highlight of the week, even if it was hard.

The meetings though, they were the true pit. Would a meeting not run if there was no pastor? Could I eat during the meeting if I hadn't eaten any meals that day? Would I be able to consume enough coffee to keep my eyes open?

Sunday slid into Monday, which slammed into Tuesday. I was always unsure if I had consumed enough caffeine to keep me going into the evening meetings. No one wants an un-caffeinated hell.

There was no mystery in meeting-hell, it was as predictable as four following three. Someone would have a mildly creative idea, and it would be shot down almost immediately. For a time, I thought it impossible for every single meeting to go like this. It wasn't until I started receiving side glances that I realized it wasn't just true, it was Truth.

It was in that institutional working truth that I was entombed. Like Lazarus, I was already gone. It was too late for me. Unlike Lazarus, Jesus couldn't save me now. I was resigned to meandering in the darkness of the hell I had helped to create for myself. I was used to it, and it was somehow quite comfortable.

It's when we get too comfortable that we don't want to leave the tomb. Why would we? We know what to expect, and while it might be death that awaits us, at least it has an endnote that we can anticipate. We understand the final chapter, and we learn to live with an end which does not have a "happily ever after." Was it too late to have something happy? Or did I just not deserve it because I wasn't enough of a pastor, mother, wife, or person to have a different ending?

Every time I wept, I took solace in knowing that Jesus wept alongside me. It wasn't enough though. I was still dying a little more with each passing day. With every passing Sunday and each staff meeting I endured. I claimed that tomb as my own.

Lazarus's story was a miracle, so why couldn't my story be miraculous? Why did my story end with dark, when his ended with light? I wasn't sure, at least not then. I realized later that I had unequivocally chosen the hell I knew, over the mystery I didn't. My four-ish days in the tomb were more like four-ish years. It did not matter how long it was as I had lost a sense of time. Time simply passed around me.

I was afraid, not of the darkness of my Lazarus tomb, but of what was on the other side. I couldn't envision my life any other way, and I couldn't see an identity past failed pastor. I kept repeating my own terrible theology, probably giving Jeeeee-sus a good twang in my mind. The string of institutional norms that had come to rule my existence drowned out what little grace I had left for myself. And the cacophonies of self-imposed and external criticisms were far too loud for me to hear the sweet sound of Jesus calling my name from the edge of the tomb, "Come out."

There were infinite tears before I realized that I preferred my cozy Lazarus tomb. With the death of my creative spirit, I couldn't even catch a glimpse of light that would help me see past the tomb's threshold. Because I had come to understand this period of my life and work as a failure, I wasn't overly excited to take on a new mysterious phase, even if it meant liberation from darkness.

Michelle Wahila

While I couldn't hear Jesus calling my name from the threshold, I could feel my body failing. I could feel the density of the graveclothes wrapped around me. With every sickness, every bizarre ailment that my body seemed to entrap, and with a fatigue that couldn't be shaken, the grave clothes tightened, securing my death.

A Prayer for Resurrection

(A palindrome liturgy – Read traditionally from the top down, Column
1. Then when finished read from the bottom up, Column 2.)

Here I am again.	Looking toward a glimmer…
It does not matter,	Wandering,
My Body gives the holy message:	Led through the darkness
Fight. Flight. Freeze.	It is enough.
A downward spiral,	What have I become?
Just some memories,	Hope.
And tears	There is no
Screaming	Screaming
There is no	And tears
Hope.	Just some memories,
What have I become?	A downward spiral,
It is enough.	Fight. Flight. Freeze.
Led through the darkness	My Body gives the holy message:
Wandering,	It does not matter,
Looking toward a glimmer…	Here I am again

A Sticky Note to Myself

My day-to-day ministry was always and forever about the meetings. I stumbled into this morning meeting like I did most meetings, disheveled after getting my kids fed and ready for school and my husband out the door in mostly clean clothes with a kiss. I had my perfectly brewed but now stone-cold coffee in one hand and my rose-colored day planner in the other.

My American sized planner had the slightly too tall, French A-4 sheets of paper sticking out the top. They were crinkled but served as a spot for my pink glitter pen to rest. I sat, anxious that I had forgotten something critical for this meeting but then remembered that nothing really happened at these meetings anyways. It was a lot of words, but very little action.

It was always the same – a man's reflection on having a productive faith that would lead us into deeper relationships with God and one another. At some point along the way, I developed the most stellar calm that kept me from guffawing out loud during these devotional moments.

I'm not sure if my silence gave me away, but silence was the safest move around that table. Any other move could spark a controversy. It was a battle that you would surely lose.

Controversy was a way of life. If it wasn't someone complaining about my hair color, it was advocating for adherence to the contractual terms that brought me to *that* place. From visa renewals to driver's licenses, every piece of paper the institution touched was poisoned with controversy.

I was at the grand door that led to The Boss's office again. I was giving myself a spirited pep talk when the Administrative Assistant gave me the go ahead to enter. I am sure she could see the fear in my eyes, or the welling tears.

I entered quietly, clearing my throat to gain his attention without words. He knew I was there, but his gaze never met mine. I wasn't sure if he couldn't look me in the eyes, or I him. My heart pounded, and I gathered the courage to speak.

"We received this bill in the mail, and I don't understand it."

"Oh, sure," he muttered, reaching toward me, snatching the paper.

"It's for the flat."

"Ok..."

I still didn't understand why I was responsible for paying it. "My terms of call cover all costs associated with the furnished flat; maybe I am misunderstanding?" I defaulted to confusion because it was easier than constant confrontation. I wanted to assume miscommunication, but it grew more difficult with each passing battle.

"Why can't you just pay it?"

"Because it's part of my compensation."

They always talked about how the apartment was part of the package. It was the flat we got; we never would have chosen it. It was the workhouse, and it cost me dearly.

Why couldn't they just pay it? It was just another small battle for them. They would wait it out to see if I caved. They would wait until the tax bill with my name on it was late. It was never their problem but always a controversy.

Beyond the meetings and all the time that I spent around that unbalanced table, I longed for conversation that allowed us to talk about hard things – not the controversies. Sharing the spaces in which we were struggling and where we found authentic happiness was my longing. I desired a place for those gathered to scream and cry or shout with elation over our victories. None of that happened around a table where not everyone had a voice.

That's the thing about voice. When it is not heard, time and again, eventually you give up trying to speak. You quit and accept your patriarchal muzzle. You allow the stifling quiet to permeate the space of your heart and head.

Sometimes, as the silence creeps in, you realize you are losing any sense of prophetic voice you ever had. Other times, you don't even realize that the sullen silence has crept into the very depths of your soul.

Though I was silent, the meeting room I was sitting in was aflutter. The chatter without depth made me wiggle uncomfortably. It wasn't what I expected from a community that claimed to center on Jesus. We kept our words politely resting on the surface. Everything was perfect there – except when it wasn't.

I rolled my glitter pen on the table, looking down in an attempt to avoid eye contact with the rest of the table-sitters. My reticence helped me cope. It kept me sane and allowed me one more day. It wasn't authentic, but it was safe.

My silent glitter-pen-rolling life was so far from what I had hoped when I arrived. I counted in my head, "1, 2, 3, 4…" I realized I was breathing rhythmically. I wondered what it would be like to simply stand up in the middle of the meeting and leave – without a word or explanation.

I thought about what the opposite end of the spectrum might be like too. Could I stand up and just scream at the top of my lungs, "WTF are we doing here if we cannot talk about things, real things, hard things?"

Michelle Wahila

With every breath in, I considered what it meant to be a pastor. One of the greatest gifts a pastor can give to her community of faith is graceful authenticity – an authentic life, lived out in various aspects of the pastoral task. Authenticity allowed me to be real from the pulpit to the boardroom, from the hospital bed to the communion table. We are called to worship in "Spirit and in truth." We are equally called to pastor that way.

I was convinced that no community of faith wanted a perfect pastor. They wanted a real one.

They have a perfect Jesus; they didn't need a perfect pastor to shepherd them. With every roll of my pink sparkly pen against that oblong table, I was determined to claim my imperfection alongside of authenticity.

Eighty-six minutes after we bowed our heads in prayer to begin, the meeting adjourned. I picked up my day planner and hooked my pink pen back into its place. I sighed at the thought of discussing nothing for so long. Pushing my prison chair back into its perfect place at that oblong table, I thought about how inauthentic I had become.

I was depleted, sure, but I was also a shell of my former self. I accepted my fate – fake smiles and skirts steeped in contention. Maybe people wanted perfect after all. The guise of perfect is more controllable.

"Thanks, have a great rest of the day." I forced out my best beauty pageant smile and darted out the door. I was assigned my worship duties for the week. I could crawl back into my wet-dog-scented cave where troubles multiplied.

I locked my door behind me and slumped into my twirling office chair. I overturned a few piles of paper the way I imagined Jesus himself to have overturned the tables in front of the temple.

"Where is it?"

I could never locate what I was looking for amidst all the papers that other people piled on my desk. I rarely used the man-sized desk in the basement, but I still locked the door to keep the papers safely in their pile. "Ahhhh there you are." I pulled off a pink sticky note from a small cube and wrote down a single word: joy.

If I could find a way to share joy, I would survive. I just needed the Spirit to help me find some. I had a picture of abundance; it was written on a hot pink sticky note. If it was written, it was real.

I did not want to give up hope that abundance was both real and vibrant. Hadn't Jesus promised life abundant? Tears started rolling down my cheeks and falling onto the paper, making my pink Post-it more of a hot pink. My imported from the U.S. permanent Sharpie ink remained steadfast in a pool of tears. If my Sharpie could do it, so could I.

Michelle Wahila

A Breath Prayer

Today I will inhale acceptance
And
I will exhale joy.

Spirit, compel me to breathe.

An Army of Sweet Bears

FROM DAY TO DAY, HOUR TO HOUR, I FELT MY SPIRIT SHRINK. I WASN'T JUST fragile, but brittle. Like a valley full of dry bones, I was a scorched pile of what once was. I sank deeper into the pit. Instead of allowing the wind of the Spirit to rush over my body bringing the breath of relief, I was drenched in dust. More dust meant more grime to settle over me and bury me deeper.

There was nothing left in the valley except my deteriorating spirit. There was equally nothing left for me in my pastoral role at that institution. The imagination that once energized my soul for creative Kindom work had long since gone. I fell into a monotonous routine of meetings, administrative tasks, and endless emails. I looked for small signs of life in the valley, but there were none.

It was lonely in the gully. I wanted to scream at the top of my lungs, but not as much as I wanted to remain under the radar. Do your job. Drink more coffee. Exist until the end of your twelve-hour day. Keep your head down, and don't let anyone see you tremble.

I was back in my office, with only moments before my next thing. I had already categorized this day as one of "the very worst ever in the history of bad." I called in reinforcements. On the very worst days, the

Haribo *l'ours d'or* were my golden bear encouragement and protectors in the valley of my office.

Stress eating loves a busy schedule. This pastor was always thankful that Holy Week led to Easter, not only because it celebrated the Resurrection of the Lord Jesus, but because it brought peanut butter eggs into existence. The holy time brought with it the sacred sweet whose ratio of peanut butter to chocolate was so much better than cups could ever be.

The bears though? They were my heroes. I imagined their little gummy faces in military straight lines guarding my desk. Their sweet dispositions were nothing but a ruse, meant to lure you into their grasp.

At every knock on my office door, not only would the hairs on my neck stand at attention, but my rainbow army would stand at attention too. Their multi-fruit goodness could make even Goliath fall. I would allow their saccharine scent to fill my nostrils with comfort. They were my best line of defense.

Prepared for battle, they kept me going. I rarely stopped for lunch, unless it was a working one. Dinner was typically a "no-go" because I was preparing for the monotonous evening meeting routine. If I stopped even my sticky sweet army and my sixth espresso couldn't keep me buzzed enough to make it through the end of the day.

"Just a little longer," as I pondered a quick run outdoors, but chose a pineapple gummy bear instead. My next meeting approached quickly. I needed to rest before round two of my day commenced.

"Bone dead tired." I used to think the term was reserved purely for old people, or maybe for pastors during Holy Week. It had become my current life's motto. It may not have been my Facebook status, but it was my life. I had to keep smiling like the rest of the staff during Easter Celebrations.

This kind of tired wasn't my once a year, "you can do it" run up to Easter. It was my daily "not doing enough to keep my head above water – take care of my family – or rejuvenate my own spiritual self – life" kinda tired.

My soul ached and the body had come to keep stride with the emptiness residing in my spirit. My limbs throbbed beyond what I could imagine as normal fatigue. I began to convince myself that the toxicity of my employment had poisoned my soul to the extent that my physical shell, the vessel in which I housed my little light, was rebelling.

"Somewhere," I thought, "I am growing a cancerous tumor." And why not? I hadn't been taking care of my clay jar. The vessel God had given me, in which I was to carry the Holy Spirit, was being neglected.

I wasn't eating well, or at all…. Maybe grabbing some packaged crap between meetings or whatever cupcake was lying around in the office. I wasn't sleeping nearly enough, and when I did, it was restless. I woke a dozen or more times during the night, remembering work that I had left undone from the day before. Exercise. What's that?

I had let go of so much: the people I loved and now missed with every shred of my being; the home we had created and recreated. I let go of things, people, and places to forge ahead and create a new path into the future. Letting go had afforded me a new role in an unknown place.

This spiritual practice was supposed to create space for the Good Lord to do a new thing in my life and the life of our family. Letting go wasn't supposed to bring you into the valley to become a brittle hot mess. I didn't sign up for more stress-eating than normal, for my body to become so fragile, or for my spirit to waste away. And yet, somehow, I had.

Surrounded by my sticky sweet army of gummy protectors, I stood up from my office chair and gazed at my beautiful rainbow-colored front line. Could my Valiant Knight be correct? Did I need to let go of this job? I could just quit.

The pineapple sergeant screamed at me, "Quitter! Deserter! Failure!" I flicked him over with my pointer finger before I plucked him up and popped him into my mouth. I snapped his little body between my teeth. "No. I am not ready to let go."

It was too much like giving up. It reeked of failure, and I wasn't ready to admit defeat because I was being bullied out of a job I felt called to do.

I just needed to think more positively about my situation. "Bless and release," I kept thinking to myself. "To everything there is a season."[1] I was stuck in battle, driven on by an army of sweetness and looking for any sign of hope.

Maybe this was all a product of my own pride; it was hurt, hidden deep inside. Whatever was keeping me in that valley, it was real.

At the same time, nothing felt real. I picked up my stapler and set it back down. I ran my fingertips over my pen jar and twirled the paper-clips around in their little container. I turned my attention from the office supplies being guarded by teeny bears to the God who I was beginning to seriously question.

"Aren't you the omnipotent one? Couldn't you have said something about all of this? A little warning would have been nice! Like before we uprooted our family and moved across the ocean..." I had tears tumbling down my cheeks (again). "Should I just quit, God?"

Quitting would have negated everything that had led me into this moment. It would have illegitimatized a legitimate call. It seemed wrong to simply let it all go. I needed to try harder because it needed to count.

I was determined to make it count. Every footstep, every faith-filled prayer and every battle scar needed to count. It was there now, on the record for all to see. I was living this. It was part of my existence, even if it was far too soon to be a piece of my story.

I wasn't going jump to the next chapter until this one was penned in full. There was no need to take a fear-filled leap into the future when I simply needed to take a faith-filled step into my present. I hadn't had a "present" in so long, I forgot what it was like. This was going to count. Overcome with the scent of sweet determination, I lined up my remaining bears for battle.

---

1. Ecclesiastes 3

An Ash Wednesday Blessing

May you be grounded through this holy season,
Remembering that you are connected to the earth,
Created of the same miraculous dust.

Wherever you plant your feet,
There is a Divine connection of creativity
That beckons you forward into the holy mystery
Of dirty, messy, miraculous creation.

Inevitably you will walk through such messiness with suffering and
grief;
Your laments will be heard by the One who placed you here with hope.
Your steps are rooted in this.
May you feel the earth beneath you,
And remember this truth.

Moving Boxes

THE IMMIGRANT LIFE IS ONE OF BEING PULLED FORWARD. IN FRANCE, there's always paperwork to be done in order to stay and call the country your own. By the time you finish one cycle of paperwork, the next begins. You are continually called toward the next thing that keeps you secure, reminding you that you're only a sojourner, even if you do call the place your home.

My own paperwork had been jumbled to incoherence by my employer, so I did not exude the gratefulness expected of me. I hemmed and hawed in words like "Contract!" and "Immigration Lawyers" but was met with disdain. I worked in the thin space of ancient rules and the privilege of my American passport, hoping it would be enough to get me in and out of the two countries I now referred to as home.

I existed in a tornado of botched paperwork and failed expectations, and I wasn't naïve in thinking that my immigrant life could remain this way. I made my own determined effort to sift and sort the mound of broken promises and bureaucracy given to me by the church. Unsuccessfully. Instead, my Valiant Knight rescued me yet again; his company took my paperwork on alongside of his. I was granted the right to work in my adopted country by the grace of an unknown HR person in company that was not my own.

Proper papers gave me a feeling of security, even if it would only remain until the next paperwork cycle. My new status came with the gift of medical care, and eventually a driver's license – pieces of privileges absent without proper paperwork. I was secure in status if not in place.

Time slipped away without a firm place in the church that had called me to serve. Three years before, we packed up our American life frantically to meet the arbitrary deadline imposed upon us by my new employer. Now, it was time to pack my church office to meet my deadline to go.

I pulled books off the snow-white bookshelves that had been a temporary home for the theological library that I moved from Pittsburgh. My theology hadn't guarded me as well as my sweet bears and anxiety. The library felt unnecessary to whisk away into our new apartment of forty-two square meters and my new (and also smaller) non-pastoral life.

I didn't have the energy anymore – for a theological or political fight, or even to move books from shelves. With a single arm swipe, I shoved the bottom shelf of books into a musty-smelling cardboard box that I found in the church attic taking up space. It was a good home for books that would take up precious space in our new, tiny dwelling.

I began to reminisce about what once was – our life that existed before. Pittsburgh was a distant life of long ago. My kids couldn't remember it, and I struggled all the same. Too much had passed, and happy memories were unfair to my present regret.

I daydreamed of what could have been. It was not a particularly helpful exercise as I was packing up my office to move. Packing was a loose term; I was throwing things at the dusty cardboard boxes. I worked until the bitter end – there was no time to pack things away with care.

It wasn't the first office I had packed. In Pittsburgh, each trinket, book, and paper placed into boxes brought fond memories of the ministry that happened there. Fond was not perfect, but it was the emotion wrapped into moments of life shared. Joy and sorrow interlaced to form the life-giving memories that are fond.

Fond memories are the memories of love and life well-lived in a particular moment in time. As I jettisoned my belongings into boxes, I gathered that I wouldn't have fond memories from this sojourn. There were memories though.

There were memories of unmet expectations and overwork – of the dampening of my spirit and gifts. There were nightmares and migraines to remind me, even if I tried to forget. Fondness was only to be found in the freedom of the moving boxes that I was shoving full.

The stained-glass ceiling in *that* place had been higher than I anticipated. When I crashed into it and fell into the pit, the patriarchy was pleased to help me question my abilities and giftings, along with my fitness for ministry. I was not fond of my tokenism or the gaslighting.

But the brief time that passed with my books on white shelves, that I was now haphazardly tossing into a box, was just long enough to erode all those truths. The things I thought I once knew of myself were, at best, a fond memory. If I had worked harder, sacrificed more, and spoken less, would I have succeeded? Could I have loved the Lord more, so that I could have been more?

I did not love Executive Jesus nearly enough to have had success in *that* place, but I loved him enough to sacrifice myself for false hope. The institution helped do the rest. There was no narrative there in which I would ever be enough. That was the truth.

I was immersed in a false narrative paraded by a false Jesus, in which everyone else fell in line. I marked my value by measures that aligned more with the system than my identity in Christ. In past lives of ministry, I would have gently placed the turquoise and brown paisley paperweight into my box marked "office" and thanked it for holding down my piles – subduing my workload. In this life, however, I looked at that paisley paperweight with disdain, wondering how I could have managed those papers better, to achieve more and be more.

I couldn't box up a false narrative along with my bookshelves. The emptiness of workaholism and institutional pride permeated every shred of my being. I placed theology books and a new paradigm for measuring self-worth into my office boxes. I left a failure at all the things – pastor, wife, and mother.

I was as worthless as the belongings that I was tossing into moving boxes. It had become second nature to hear the words of failure and write them onto my heart. I embodied the despair.

Like the office supplies piling up in the box, the emotion of leaving as a failure was accumulating in my soul. The angst of not knowing what was next was also, ever so quietly, whispering to me. The moving of the boxes couldn't have come sooner. But moving out of my vocation, which had been an integral part of my identity before the parts labelled wife and mother, could wait.

Tears were resting at the edges of my eyes again. I yearned for something hopeful to be found amidst the clanking of binders, books, and office supplies. My despair was met with silence, and I rummaged through the box to find an unopened package of gummy bears.

Sitting on my office floor, I continued shoving books into boxes while slipping the oh-so protective bears into my mouth. How had I gone so far astray? I was a fragmented mess of a human, having trouble packing boxes to move. No wonder I was incapable of claiming my identity as a child of God, much less a shepherd of God's people.

I sat amidst boxes and let the tears become reality. They sprinkled the musty boxes in a baptism of grief. I was being pulled into what was next, like it or not; my immigrant heart knew it was well past time. Sojourners can never get too comfortable because the grace of moving comes before hearts get too boxed in to move again.

A Liturgy for Moving

Send me on my way.
The cardboard boxes have been filled,
Memories packed with care.
I have saved those pieces of life
That I pray will serve me as I go.
I have released those things
That have served neither here nor there.
I leave behind pieces of my heart.
They may stay in the company of friends.
I take with me love gifted here.
May it fill my heart in times of future loneliness.
In a new place that feels far from home,
May I be placed with grace.
Root me into open arms.
Open my heart to receive
The people and places waiting for me
That it might come to be called home.
Send me on my way.

The Miracle of Pasta

I STOOD IN THE KITCHEN DIRECTLY ACROSS FROM MY VALIANT KNIGHT. I could touch him and both sides of our galley kitchen. I leaned against the plastic wood-like countertop twirling our espresso tower as he prepared dinner and stirred the garlic infused red sauce on the stove.

It was one of those rare evenings when we were all together. It was Sunday and that meant an Italian feast. He was preparing pasta, just as he had a million and one times before on a Sunday evening.

He was stirring the pot of sauce on the stovetop every few minutes. The scent of olive oil and garlic filled my nostrils. He stirred and I twirled.

"How did we get here?"

"A plane."

"No kidding," I tittered back. He was always such a kidder. "I mean here, in this unhappiness."

"Is that where we are, really?"

"Maybe I just don't have enough faith to do this job."

At a time when I felt like I needed more faith, I found myself with a feeling of less. I was questioning every decision I had ever made. Crying out to God in my nightly crying sessions, I pondered what I had done to get our family into this position.

Why was it that I sold all my things and moved my family across the ocean? Was it for a call or an institution? Was it for God at all?

I had ten thousand questions about life. I didn't feel like I could answer any of them. I asked my spouse instead. I looked to him for answers to my questions because he was always so logical. Sometimes I hated his logical engineer's brain. It was always so damn right.

"It's not forever," he said with a metered tone of voice that made me hate logic even more.

"I knoooooow." Responding with my sarcastic Valley girl flavor that he probably hated as much as I despised logic.

"Having faith doesn't mean having perfect."

Damn it, he was right again. Sometimes he reminded me that because he was an engineer, he was, in fact, always right. I didn't believe that, but I trusted what he had just said so concretely that it was disorienting.

"But it hurts. It hurts so much." I didn't need to add that. He knew how much our existence hurt. Our lives had dramatically changed and looked vastly different than we had imagined them to be. Though I understood the words my Valiant Knight said to me, my present hurt too much to contemplate and to believe. Watching him prepare an Italian pasta feast was much the same as it had always been, but its similarity to our former life stung.

———

Some hurts never go away completely, wounds become scars that remind you that you have been buried in darkness. And when you acknowledge the scars, you must admit that it hasn't all been perfect.

Perfect wasn't my goal. I didn't want the #dreamjob or the #blessed #dreamlife. I wanted real. And real felt like a very rare form of love – the kind we aren't always brave or vulnerable enough to live into...

But I was certain it existed. I caught its aroma in a pot filled with pasta sauce.

Part of me wanted to say I was wasting my life in *that* place, but I knew it wasn't entirely true. I was learning what I did not want in my life – to let go of perfection, the politics, and the constraints of the patriarchy. I was learning to snub the old boys' club and Executive Jesus.

The kind of love that is brave enough to be transparent and defiant enough to brush off my perfectly well-paying job in the posh *7th arrondissement* where Executive Jesus lived, that's the love that wins. It is all-encompassing and dynamic, but it requires courage that I didn't think I possessed.

It is why authentic true and genuine love is so miraculous. It brings bravery to make the impossible possible and can penetrate our most rigid human walls that we have built around us. Love seeps into our darkest moments bringing healing. It is a miracle.

The questions, the hurt and the scars helped me realize that I was more "out" than "in" as far as the institutional church went. Authenticity required more from me than a perfect Sunday smile and pandering to the patriarchy and Executive Jesus. I was learning that the risky business of love was the work of the church, and it wasn't about boxing in what love should look like. I was more misfit than management, and it was a miracle.

For all the times my Valiant Knight wailed, "You can just leave!" I finally started to believe him.

We may have been preparing pasta, but we were learning love. We were learning that rules were meant to be broken to make a way forward and that love resides in the nitty-gritty of life. It's the kind of love that isn't afraid to get dirty, even if it means picking up the messy pieces of someone's broken heart.

My conclusion was wrong. It wasn't about having more faith. It was about having just enough faith to figure out what to do next, together. God wasn't asking us to give more of ourselves or to give something we didn't yet possess just to "make it."

"Have faith that we will get through this together."

He stirred and I twirled.

"Buuuuuuut this is hell."

"You can't hold hands in hell. It's too hot."

I grabbed my Valiant Knight's hand turning him toward me and snuggled into my favorite spot on his chest. So much of our existence had been swallowed by our circumstances. My heart was stirred, and my thoughts twirled. Life together wasn't perfect, but it was precious.

I didn't understand why everything felt heavy and painful – even our normal Sunday pasta dinner. Maybe it was the fragrance of tomato sauce wafting toward me, but I was strangely convinced that it was going to be ok. Either way, the strong scent of garlic and hope miraculously filled the void of that moment.

A Prayer for Times of Uncertainty

Spirit,
You who are unyielding love,
Embrace me.

Holding onto the Hosannas

EVERY STAFF MEETING FELT LIKE I WAS LIVING OUT THE JUXTAPOSITION OF Palm Sunday theology. There were elated shouts of joy contrasted with the people's cry of "Hosanna" around that oblong table. Amidst the planning, the details, and the theological catch phrases of the week shouted with elation, "Hosanna" could be heard in the murmur of those who sat but did not speak. The contrast was stark, yet unnoticeable to some who came to the table. While a few enjoyed a parade, others of us cried out, "Save us, please! Hosanna."

Everybody loves a parade. There were plenty of parades to go around in *that* place – but only for a certain few. If you weren't the protégé forget it; if you weren't in the boy's club, you weren't getting the triumphal entry... Only the elite received the crash of cymbals for their entrance. The rest of us had to create our own entrance, our own way, and our own quiet paths.

I didn't need to see the palm branches waving in my face. I needed the Hosanna cries of salvation. I didn't need the boardroom-sitting Executive Jesus to put on a good show at a staff meeting. I longed for the Jesus who would go with me to the dark places of the institution that felt abusive in power, crushed my spirit, and were outright vain.

They told me that it was my fault – for not balancing work and family well. I was a three-legged stool, they said. I was never going to balance enough to stand tall. Please save me, Jesus, from my unbalance.

In and through all the balancing, I thought I caught a glimpse of the Jesus I once knew. This Jesus wanted me to be me. And I was a balance: pastor, wife, mother. This Jesus wanted more than an institutional imbalance of power would allow.

My calling was not going to be stabilized in a place that wouldn't allow a mother to mother or a pastor to pastor. I was never going to be me in *that* place, with Executive Jesus looking over my shoulder. I was always going to disappoint and be disappointed; I could never seem to follow the rules well enough.

I entered the church doors as a rule follower. I could have given Executive Jesus a run for his money. I crossed the T's and dotted all the I's. I could feel the love of the precious saints who shepherded me into ministry ushering me back out the church doors. One of those saints would often remind me that the path to ministry meant, "Get your ticket punched."

What I would often forget is the phrase he spoke next: "…and get out." He never meant get out of the church, he meant get on with it. Get on with your life, and the ministry to which you have been called. It meant not getting bogged down in the committee work of crossing T's and dotting I's. Get your ticket punched, fulfill your requirements, and then do more. Get on with the holy work to which you have been called.

I dreamed of leaving *that* place and leaving the rules of Executive Jesus behind too. I came in as a rule follower, but I would leave a rule breaker. Love doesn't follow the rules. Love brings abundance to the present tense – and will break all the rules to do so.

Time and again, when I wasn't putting on a good enough show for Executive Jesus, I had the privilege of sitting at the table to be told how well I was failing. Sometimes, my colleague got to be there as well. At least I wasn't alone.

Meeting after meeting brought more of the same. There were trumpets and banners for some and a vacuum of silence for the rest of us. The silence was cold, but the table chatter was colder.

Occasionally, though, the words would come my way.

I wanted to duck, shrink or shout back, but I would just sit as the words pummeled my heart. I was "self-aggrandizing," yet also "unaware." I was befuddled at being both, but the words told me it was true.

Once, in a carefully worded post-meeting email, I gathered the courage to say the words, "I felt belittled..." Documented so it was real. I took a deep breath and hit "send." I instantly wished I hadn't.

It was The Boss's day off, but he probably read the email the minute it hit his inbox, and five minutes later my phone rang. In a flurry of words that barely fit together he told me of his disappointment. "It should never have been sent." He said it so well that I almost believed him. He was correct. How dare I feel belittled by words of truth, that were there to make me better at my job? Never mind that my colleague heard them; they were words that needed to be said. I supervised him, so surely he already knew how inadequate I was?

My email held words that need not be spoken, or so I was told. I should have had tougher skin. I should have taken the time to have a conversation.

But now my email would remain in his inbox, kept in my file "just in case."

I wasn't sure if "just in case" would ever come, but I feared it just the same, wrapping it into my nightmares with all the rest. I imagined my file growing alongside those of all the others who dared to disappoint. I had failed Executive Jesus again.

Executive Jesus was so shiny and well put together, but he didn't give me hope. I needed the Jesus who was heading toward the darkness of the cross. After Palm Sunday, the disciples' cries of Hosanna all shrank away. Hosanna was erased from their lips as Christ was denied, betrayed, humiliated, and handed over. As the "Hosannas" from the crowd faded, the disciples fell away, and Jesus was left alone.

I wanted a Jesus who wasn't afraid to be alone, a Savior who wouldn't shy away from a dark reality, and a Hosanna that could resound through my soul. I needed to know that when all the disciples shrank away – when I shrank away – Jesus would remain steadfast.

The dark and lonely places are exactly where the "Hosannas" should resound. Those places were the only abundance I felt. My own cries of "Save me, please" were many.

I hoped for a Jesus gentle enough to embrace my hosannas. I knew I couldn't hold them alone, but I needed to let them linger a while in my heart. They needed to stay with me, because if they were there, they could give me purpose. I could make the rest of the journey. The hosannas weren't about the parade, they were full of hope for liberation.

Hosannas are a call to justice and to love. They are a call to "more." Christ carried the hosannas all the way to the cross, I only needed Him to carry mine for a moment. Around the weighted table of the institution, I frantically reached to collect all my hosannas, hoping Jesus would hold them, even if just for a while.

Sure, I got my ticket punched, I fulfilled the long and arduous process of seminary and ordination, but those rules did not define me or limit me. They weren't what made me. Love made me.

The truth is that I always saw myself inside the church. It was home for me. I grew up there. I was baptized, confirmed, married, ordained, and installed there. I never imagined that this same institution that called me would be the one that also released me. Nevertheless, with much weeping and gnashing of teeth, I eventually did lay down my robe and my stole. At the time, I believed my professional career in ministry was finished, but hanging in the balance was my life as wife and mother that I simply could not continue to sacrifice.

Holding Hosannas: An Intercession for Oneself

You are the God who can bring life from death,
Who can stir up dry bones with breath,
And who can infuse hope into the deepest void.

Save me, please?

Hold my weeping
And my heart;
Hold my hosannas.

But if I must linger in sorrow a bit longer,
Trying to reclaim life,
Trying to breathe,
Trying to grasp hope,

Weep with me, please?

Sitting in Rage and Hope on Sunday

SOME SUNDAYS I WOULD SIT IN WORSHIP GRIEF-STRICKEN, OTHER SUNDAYS were more a combination of rage, angst, and general sadness. My Sunday mood was a byproduct of the work week. You could be belittled during the week, but on Sundays we sat in our pews and smiled.

I forced a small grin again. I was sure that I was a little frowny, knowing I would hear the same atonement-centered message again this week. Though it did remind me how much I needed a Savior. He would save me from never being enough for this place.

My eyes were tired. I hadn't slept enough, but I sat at attention while the announcements were given. The talking heads spoke. After sliding in how many countries were represented in the worshipping community, we were headed toward the diversity finale. For the finale we received the great welcome. "All are welcome here; you are welcome here." I knew it wasn't true.

I wanted to throw something or scream, but I was in worship. I sat silently instead – like a faithful woman should.

I have great affection for the pastors who spent time encouraging, training, and pushing me forward in ministry. Whenever I sat in the pew, I sat with the long history of saints who had given so much to teach, love, admonish, and encourage me. Any real faithfulness I had was a result of their investment in me.

When I sat in the dark wooden pew in *that* place, and I thought about those who had given so much to me, I never felt like my anger toward the institution was justified. Or maybe it was. It was just that I had been told so many times that it was not.

At some point, I realized that the critique I was attempting to voice about the institution was not entirely rage. It may have been the under-pinning, but it wasn't the source. It was coming from a place of hope – hope for something more.

As I sat my exhausted rear-end in the pew that Sunday morning, I didn't think I felt hopeful, but I could feel fury building from deep inside. The crescendo of the organ served to stir my faith and my indignation.

With the organ's final note, I envisioned myself rising from my front pew position and walking out of the church doors. I understood why people were leaving the global church in droves. Amidst scandal and hypocrisy, I didn't blame them for leaving and never looking back. I wondered if that would be my own fate.

It was finally the end; it had been a rather normal Sunday service. We were recessing out of the sanctuary in our long, black, academic robes. I was wearing a mostly red stole quilted with a rainbow of colors in the shape of flames that draped over my shoulders. It was as if my outside was adorned with what my inside felt.

I didn't storm out of the church doors that Sunday. I walked the recessional with all the pomp and circumstance required for a red-stole festival day. Slowly we marched, two by two, down the lengthy middle aisle. I tiptoed around the brass grates on the floor that could entrap my black kitten-heels. I had become proficient at tiptoeing around complications.

I marched in perfect stride next to my male colleague. I glanced over at him, wondering what he was thinking about. I thought that maybe he also desired to exit through those wooden doors ahead of us and keep walking. Maybe if he did, I wouldn't be so alone.

I couldn't put my finger on why I kept plodding along the same course that kept me squarely in line. Sunday was the perfect picture of what life had become. With each kitten-heeled step, I was slowly following the leader in my black robe. Even with all the tiptoeing, I found my heart being pulled toward the institution that I sort of despised.

In between glances toward my colleague, I was looking into the eyes of all the saints I was passing on my way out of the church. Some had smiles, and others had sad, tired eyes like my own. Maybe they had a fiery rage building inside too.

I stopped at the portico where the big black gates separated the outside from the inside. I stood at the edge looking outward toward the outside of the stone church. I stood in line, like a faithful woman should. As the organ postlude came to a dramatic final note, I took my spot at the threshold of the imposing black gates of the church.

I stood between spaces – the outside and the inside. Today I hadn't run out. I placed my kitten-heels on the edge and stood up taller than I had in a long while. Though I held my head high, my heart was broken – grieving a place I thought existed but did not. I wallowed plenty in my broken expectations too.

The wallowing passed, like it did every Sunday. This Sunday, however, it was replaced by something else. Was it rage? No, I had that every Sunday. What was this warm but not quite fiery feeling inside of me?

In a dreamy kind of flash, I pictured the mentors, family and friends who encouraged me in ministry. I thought of all the saints who had loved me into that place. I knew their support helped guide me into this spot; today, I believed they could also love me out of it.

Something shifted in me on that most normal of Sundays. Though I sat in the same pew, heard the same announcements, prayed the same prayers, and sang the same hymns, something changed. Transformation is sneaky that way. Sometimes, even when we're at our end, we are still becoming.

Maybe it was the act of placing my feet at the threshold with my head held high that transformed my anger into something else. Was this hope? Perhaps I simply found my proper spot – not outside the church, but not quite inside either. The threshold was the place where I was meant to be.

―――――――

I knew that I was not going to dig my heels in and stay forever. Envisioning an end helped me tolerate my middle. With that vision, my broken heart began to open just enough. It was just enough to reflect something loving and a little less judgmental in my middle.

I stood at the edge of the gated portico, with just enough.

The people were pouring out of the church doors leaving worship. Unlike me, they were stepping over that threshold and into the world. I looked into their eyes and prayed for every passing person. I saw love and sometimes pain in a stream of passing saints, and it was beautiful.

Somehow it was also enough. I was still rage-filled and grief-stricken. But what kept me leaning toward hope and away from (metaphorically) burning it all to the ground, was the beautiful.

Hope was beautiful.

Hope told me that there was something beyond this ending. I wasn't ready to claim a story that told me I needed to suffer to "come out better." That's an especially dangerous road to martyrdom for a well-educated, white, cisgender, heterosexual woman. With every given privilege, I need not spiral down that path. Growth was not synonymous with martyrdom, and hope sprung forth despite me.

Instead, I found that hope reminded me that having just enough can be beautiful. I had no idea what could come after this ending. I only knew that I was tired of sitting in that wooden pew on Sundays, full of rage. There was too much beautiful around me for that.

The church continued to empty. I shook hands and gave hugs. There was even a *bise* or two. Somewhere amid greeting those flooding out of the church, I realized that I was whispering "Goodbye," to each person who passed me on the portico.

That Sunday, I said the first of what would be a long string of farewells.

I stepped down one step from the threshold. Inching my way closer to the outside world away from the inside of the sanctuary, I sighed. I wasn't going to let the beautiful pass by me.

It wasn't my academic robe, the processionals, or recessionals, or even a salad spinner mix of sermony-words that made Sunday, Sunday. It was the people. The movement of saints out of the building and into the real world reminded me that I had hope in a living, moving faith. It was a compelling story for an average Sunday; one I thought I had most certainly read before.

Michelle Wahila

Prayer for Knitting Together a Broken Heart

You knit me together before I came into the universe, but my time in this world has put me in knots and my threadbare soul is tired. Weave back together the pieces of my broken heart. I trust that you can mend the places where I am being ripped apart. Intertwine my life with love, that I might be reminded of the tapestry I am still becoming.

Running (Away)

Living and working in the same building meant that there were several days per week when I did not see the outside of the church building. It was hard to remember what Paris was like on the outside of that stone building with imposing wooden doors. But if I had the chance to exit, I would run.

Running kept me grounded. It kept me sane in what was the untethered world of institutional politics. It was the only thing grounding me. Feeling the pavement beneath my pounding feet allowed me to claim what little life I had left within me.

With every stride, I knew that I was still alive, and that somehow the dry bones hadn't won. I was still comprised of muscles, sinews, and tendons. Every rhythmic breath reminded me that I was still breathing – in-and-out, even if I was gasping for air. With every mile ticked, I knew that I had the ability to move forward. I couldn't be stuck in one place when I was running.

It was practically the only spiritual discipline I had kept. Prayer felt distant because I had lost my voice. Worship became a vacant show. Devotionals were empty because so was my heart.

The connections of heart and head felt out of sorts. To intentionally connect the physical with the mental and spiritual was life-giving in a time when all the things around me felt life-taking. I could breathe. I had to breathe, or I couldn't run.

I could take in the quiet of the sleeping city and remember that I lived in one of the chicest metropolises in the world. My bestie and I would begin our running trek so early in the morning that part of the city was not yet sleeping, while the other part was just waking to begin the day. It was the Paris of the in between, and a juxtaposition that pointed me toward the delicate balance of life I was missing.

——————

As we ran past the market stalls, we would see them setting up before dawn. Somehow, seeing the day ahead of these market vendors was refreshing. There was abundance in the displays being set.

Like a parade of hope, every piece of perfectly cultivated French fruit, every delightfully rich *légume*, and every exquisite Parisian posy sat enticing market goers to bring them home. It was good that I couldn't run with produce. I was enticed and drawn in by the sights, smells, and sounds of the *marché* before dawn.

Just after the market, we came to the portion of Paris that hadn't yet slept. The club-goers, stumbling out from their wild night, drunk and still yearning to get lucky, were pouring out into the streets after the club's final call. They were, perhaps, less tempting than the rainbow of produce at the market, but infinitely more colorful.

It wasn't uncommon for drunk men to start running after us. We weren't breaking any speed records after all. Our slow pace and fluorescent runner's attire enticed them in the same way the produce caught our gaze in the market. "*Allons-y!*" I would yell, and the club kid would normally take up stride. It wouldn't last though; our slow pace was a deception of perseverance that could outlast even the most dedicated raver.

This liminal space was neither day nor night, the city both not yet sleeping and not yet entirely awake. And I was somehow running through the in between place. It was a mirror of my present in the church.

My transitional moment had come – I was leaving but not yet... I was still bound to the institution but so ready to go. My life even now reflected that of the club kids who barely slept at night, and the market vendors, who woke early to complete the day's tasks.

I prepared my running clothes the night before our long runs, so as to not disturb my sleeping soulmate. I would tiptoe around the flat, as I always did, gearing up for the three or four hours ahead of me. Silently, I took inventory of all my power gels and water bottles. Navigo pass, credit card, house key – check, check, check. I had everything I needed to go out the door.

If I made it to the end, I knew I would be rewarded with the buttery goodness of a flakey croissant and warm frothy latte. The gourmet finish line would be worth the hours of painful miles. I hoped my finish line would be worth it.

With every passing mile or kilometer (I hadn't yet converted to the metric system, but my bestie kept me on track), the goal of patisserie became more achievable and real. I longed to make it to the end of my pilgrimage where I could sit and pay homage to St. Arbucks with a cup of delight in my hands.

Toward the end of those hours, there was what my bestie described as a gradual downhill. "Great, it's all downhill from here." Downhill isn't always gentle. Every niggle, tweak and twiggle of pain shows up. You may have ignored the pain for hours, months or years. But downhill will remind you it's there.

My finish line felt like a mirage that would never be reached. I was certain I would wander thirsty, forever.

It was the cruelest descent of my life. I had ignored the pain in my body and soul until it ached all over. The pounding of my day-to-day existence became excruciating and remained that way until the bitter end. I continued to put one foot in front of the other, but I was shuffling.

I knew I would be able to finish now, but the race took its toll on me. It was not glutes and ankles, but it burned. There wouldn't be cheers or a parade of confetti, but still I would cross the finish line, exhale, and know that I was closer to the Divine love than I had ever been in my life, though I worried the damage would claim all of me.

At the end, I stood on the sanctuary stage as words were spoken to the church on my behalf. No different than most days – but with more bite than fair – a story was told, and I smiled. I was so close to the end; I could smile.

I remember the words, "She challenged me," which were meant just as they sounded. My Valiant Knight stood by my side, with his arm around my back so he could pinch me. His fingers squeezed the small of my back, but the pain did not deter me from clenching my teeth with the resolve to leave and never look back.

A story that waved goodbye as well as good riddance, it lacked as much truth as empathy. Told with a smile, the people applauded, and I was numb to the pain of all that was held but not spoken. That was enough. I wanted no more; it was time to set my face toward the door.

———

Sometimes, in the moments past midnight but before dawn, it felt like I wouldn't be able to go out the door. A shot of espresso would help get me going. The nectar offered me new life or at least a chance at finishing. I only wanted a chance to finish it all well. I would hold a small pink ceramic cup between my hands and give thanks for what was to come.

I would lace up my sneakers and decide I could do it. Laces were tied; there was no sense in not going. I wanted to go after all.

Running kept me going in the time in between, until the moment when I finally could run out of those church doors. And the bitter aroma filled my nostrils – I just had to go.

A Liturgy of Loss

If you have a candle to light, you can light it to begin this ritual. As you light your candle, try to focus on your breath. Invite the Holy Spirit into this moment. Let the breath of life fill your nostrils. Breathe in through your nose, filling your chest, and all the way into your tummy. Take a big deep breath. This is the breath of life. As you exhale, allow your body to settle into the breath more deeply. Breathe out those things that you wish to release. Focus on the rhythm of your breathing – slow, calm, deep. Breathe and be silent.

We light a candle for all that has been lost.

We begin by grieving all that holds darkness for us in this moment.

We grieve the loss of a life that we expected and a present that we cannot fully comprehend.

We allow ourselves to feel the sorrow that comes with seeing a present in which we were unprepared to live.

We grieve the brokenness of our relationships, and the ways that our present may have magnified the hardship of severed relations.

For all that we have loved and lost, given, and not received, we grieve.

We allow ourselves to acknowledge the future that will not come to pass. We remember the dreams that have been crushed, the expectations that have crumbled, and the hopes that have been dashed within us.

We grieve all of the places that remain longing in our hearts.

We simply allow the grief to "be." It is uncomfortable. We shift around in this discomfort because maybe this is the first time that we have acknowledged our own heartache.

[*A Moment of Silence*]

When we are ready and able, we will release these things.

We breathe in life, even as we hold and acknowledge grief.

Now, we exhale and release the things we hold in grief.

137

Michelle Wahila

We let go because we do not need to hold them.
We know that Christ holds all for us, and when we are ready,
   He will be there – for He has been with us all along.
Even in this moment, we embrace and give thanks for sweet
   memories that will continue to lead us into expectation.
The God who created out of nothing, can and will create some-
   thing new in us – even in this moment.

The Gift of an Orthopedic Boot

DECEMBER THE TWENTY-FOURTH WAS THE END. IT WOULD BE THE LAST service, my last day in the office, and the last time I needed to nod "yes," when I really wanted to scream, "No!" I was going out the wooden doors, into new life. I felt brave. I felt bold. I felt ready.

What I did not expect was the rush of emotion that swelled as I watched the lighting of the Christ candle that Christmas Eve. I didn't expect to care so much. I had spent so long trying to avoid the thinly veiled church politics and walking mouse-like around the church building.

The singing of "Silent Night," rang loudly through my soul. I sniffled and snorted my way through the benediction, looking out at all the little lights shining so brightly. Every person there in that sanctuary mattered to the Most Holy God, the One who came down to dwell among us.

Every person, except me, I thought.

When I walked out of that sacred space, I was going to snuff out the little light I was holding, in protest to the God who felt so absent during my time in *that* place. I would blow it out and watch the smoke rise like a lament in a refuge that should have kept my flame ablaze. I couldn't bring myself to do it. The house lights came back on.

139

Michelle Wahila

Worshippers exited while "Joy to the World" exuberantly played on the organ, and my little light flickered on, shining in a dark place.

I hobbled out of the sanctuary on the broken foot that had come as an early Christmas gift to me – even my final exit wasn't as grand as I anticipated. There was no parade, and I couldn't whoosh myself out slamming the church doors behind me. Instead, I hobbled out, with all the stuff I had with me for the long day – approximately three bags worth of stuff – and I two-stepped down the stairs shakily with my bags on one arm and my cup of eggnog in the other.

I was hop-stepping down the front stairs of the church when my young colleague caught a glimpse of my ridiculous struggle. He smirked but offered to hop me home, a few blocks from the church where I once lived and worked. Part of my transition out, had been moving out – not far, but far enough.

I only had to make it a few blocks. I assured him I would be okay then smiled in "not really okay." And he held out his arm for me to interlock mine into.

It was after midnight. The city was quiet but there were still people making their way here or there. The twinkling decorative lights still illuminated the streets with the proper amount of cheer for Christmas Eve.

The last church service finished with cookies and eggnog. Once the last dish was away, I was released to go, to begin the wrapping I had been putting off. There were bows, scissors, and my three sleeping people at home.

Though midnight had come and gone, it didn't feel different. The twenty-fourth had become the twenty-fifth, and it did not yet feel like change. I was finished but still trying to leave, with my orthopedic boot slowing me down.

140

It was a crime against Christmas, the way it all came to pass. I had moved our house elf, Piccolo, to his new hiding spot, creating elvish mischief for my boys to find in the morning. I gave him a hiding spot just past the couch. I tucked him into his new place, and myself into bed.

A combination of almost sound sleep and screeching little voices startled me awake the next morning. "Mommy, come! We found Piccolo." Without thinking, I jolted out of bed toward the pesky elf.

Before I knew what was happening, my knees were buckling, and I collapsed onto the floor. I had only moved, at most, two steps out of bed. Somehow, in the rush of elven excitement, I caught my foot awkwardly on the couch. I could feel heat tingling through my body from head to now mangled toe.

When I went to stand back up, I began to faint and sat back down before my spinning head went dark. I came back around with one rather worried Baby Chicken clucking over me. "Mom, are you ok?"

"Well, not really. Could you get me some water? I am feeling rather dizzy."

"Ok Mommy, I'll get it. Where's Dad?"

"He already left for work because he needs to be back in time to take care of you so I can go to work tonight. I have a worship service tonight."

My Valiant Knight was over an hour away from home and couldn't rescue me this time. Calling him was not worth it. I had limited time to figure how to get my kids to school, and (probably, if there was time) myself to the hospital.

Once I had a chance to think about what I needed to do next, my foot was already a lovely shade of purple, complete with copious amounts of swelling. I looked down at the puffy violet mess that I had gotten myself into. I always managed to make such a mess of things.

I had my kiddo fetch my phone and I began dialing every number of the people I knew in the neighborhood. When you've lived and worked in the same place for years, your neighbors are your colleagues. And your colleagues are busy, or have their own family to care for, and at Christmas time everyone is caught in Advent busyness.

No one answered. I didn't even know who I could call at seven in the morning and not lose a friend. Not that there were many to lose.

I knew my younger male colleague would be sleeping but I was getting increasingly desperate, and anxious about getting the boys to school. I was out of friends to call, but with the anxiety and pain hitting a crescendo, I dialed. Even as I was hitting the numbers on the phone screen, I thought to myself, "He is going to kill me."

To my surprise and delight, he answered his cell. "You're lucky."

"Why?"

"Because I was up all night playing my new PS4."

"Oh my God. I need your help! Please! I am broken."

Probably the truest words I had spoken in months. I was broken. The foot was only a constant nagging, and now purple, reminder.

When my friend looked at me on Christmas Eve, I was sure he could see my brokenness, not just my preposterous foot injury. My quiet exit from the church on the eve of the twenty-fifth came with laughter, and a sense of fragility. With my arm wrapped in his, I was reminded that Christ was birthed into a cold dark world, in which we are called to be the touch of Christ.

As I made my clumsy way home with his help, I hummed "Silent Night" in my head again. I hadn't been able to shake that blessed holy night out of my mind. Maybe I started humming aloud, because my colleague glanced at me, and we giggled. It was all so preposterous.

At the end of an outlandish story was a touch of hope. It was there with me in the security of an embrace keeping me steady enough not to spill my eggnog while making my way home. I hung on tightly and hopped home on one foot.

We ushered in Christmas together that year, quietly in the darkness. It wasn't with the pomp and circumstance of trumpets or bells, but Christmas came. Though I had shepherded in Christmas in a stained-glass sanctuary not an hour earlier, Christmas came humbly on an almost deserted side street in Paris.

Christmas came with the humiliation of brokenness, not just an orthopedic boot. It came without the whistles and bells of a grand exit. And enough silence to honor my sorrow.

As I hobbled the serene streets, aglow with twinkling lights, I allowed my tired body to relax a little. I clung tightly onto the arm that offered me support. For the first time in a long time, I allowed another human being to help me.

As my colleague hopped me home that Christmas Eve, he teased me about my ridiculous orthopedic boot, and we laughed out loud at my plight. My plans of rattling the church doors in exodus were thwarted by absurdity. I left in mouse-like hopping style, like the tiptoeing that kept me safe in *that* place.

I couldn't even tiptoe around now. I was forced to wait patiently to be liberated from that ugly orthopedic boot. It was an Advent of sorts. Big plans became much less grandiose, as I sat on my sofa watching Netflix with a peppermint mocha and the hope of healing rapidly. But we simply cannot will bones or hearts that are broken to heal with haste.

Michelle Wahila

A Liturgy of Brokenness

If you have a candle to light, you can light it to begin this ritual. As you light your candle, take note of how your body is feeling. Allow tears to freely come if they are there. The Psalmist reminds us that God has collected all our tears in a bottle. God has recorded our pain. Our sorrows are known. Consider your tears an offering to the God who knows you completely.

If tears, at any time, roll down your cheeks, let them also remind you that you remain the salt of the earth – even if your tasks of faith appear to have changed into something very different.

For now, your task is simply to be with the God who knows and loves you.

Breathe.
Your sorrows are known.
Breathe.
You are loved.
Breathe.

We light this candle for all our brokenness.

We look within ourselves and recognize the stirring of our hearts; it seems to only highlight the places where we already feel cracked. We see chaos around us; we are overwhelmed.

For all of the places where we need healing, and for life's messiness, which limits us from God's wholeness, we allow the light to flicker in – if only but for a moment. We are satisfied with this moment, pressing ourselves into it. That's enough, and it is full.

We acknowledge the pain of loss, which makes us feel so broken: loss of people we love, loss of trust in those with power, loss of jobs, loss of health, loss of security, loss of normalcy, loss of the little things that bring us joy.

We acknowledge and embrace the pain, O God, and we offer it to you, asking that into our wounded hearts and open hands you will place the gift of peace, edging us ever so slightly toward you and toward the gift of healing.

Wedded in Holy Discontent

I wondered if my discontent was holy. Trying to pray, I questioned whether my uneasiness was the Spirit pushing me toward the brink of something brand new, anxiety, or indigestion. I wasn't confident that the prayer was lodging my complaint in the right department, up there with Executive Jesus.

Though I had left the church behind, Executive Jesus hadn't seemed to loosen his grip on my heart. He was still right above me, looking down, reminding me what a complainer I had been. It was a familiar voice, and the only one I seemed to have resonating through my soul.

Lord knows I could have used a good dose of holy discontent. My rubbish prayer life came up empty again, and I was certain Executive Jesus had filed my complaint in the round. That's where most of my ideas had gone before anyway.

In my less-than-holy discontent, I was settling my rear into the sofa when I saw a message appear on my phone screen. I hadn't talked to that dear soul in a while; it would be good to catch up. A conversation would quiet Executive Jesus for a second, at least that's what I hoped.

It was simple and quick. A couple to marry, turned down by the church, could I help a friend of a friend? The wedding was coming; I would have to prepare. I wasn't sure I remembered how to pastor.

But my typing was fast, frenzied, and furious – how was it that this became true? Preposterous! I refused to believe it, but there it was on my screen. Blessing was thwarted by Executive Jesus; the rules are the rules, or so we'd always been told.

If holy discontent exists, it found me on my couch. One message became one wedding that became four weddings then five…

The thought of blessing being barricaded by the church burdened my heart. But I was no longer bound to Executive Jesus. Instead, I stood in the back garden of Notre Dame on a blustery but sunny November Tuesday, to bless two amazing humans. Unwelcome in the stone sanctuary I once thought of as home, the great cathedral's spire stood as a witness to love. In the midst of blessing, I dug my peep-toes into the space between holy discontent and what came next. Fifty weddings turned into one hundred, and I was reborn, wedded to holy discontent.

I knew what had come before, and it was the source of my rage-filled self. We aren't meant to be boxed into a small existence. And the ministry of the church was never supposed to be confined to four walls with stained glass. I thought Jesus had sent us out into the world. Ironically, I spent a great deal of my existence inside those sanctuary walls, discontent.

I forgot that I could walk down the street and see some of the greatest monuments and art in the world. I failed to remember that I could pop around the corner to purchase the best baguette, wine, and cheese on the planet. I didn't recall why I thought I heard God's call on my life to move here in the first place. The longer I spent inside those cold stone walls, the more I forgot about my sense of call.

The sun shone down onto a tall pair of gentlemen dressed in perfectly tailored suits. They embraced me in a hug that almost suffocated my petite frame. We turned toward the spire and admired her beauty. Notre Dame was a magnificent and holy setting for a wedding.

I was mesmerized by the marriage scene of which I was somehow a part. There was no scenario in my former state that would have led me to believe that this moment was possible. But God's call has a way of blossoming in the space between the untamed and the sacred.

The taller of the two pulled up his pantleg, so that we could, all three, admire his argyle socks. We laughed at the holy mystery of argyle. "Every moment holy," I thought to myself as I appreciated blue and red argyle and the two smiling men who I had just married.

A moment drenched in sunlight in Notre Dame's back garden was as sacred as any service of worship I had ever officiated before... I was just as much a pastor in that sweet moment of quiet, as I had been in those moments at the front of the neogothic sanctuary. I had just quietly forgotten my own sacred identity.

When we forget who we are, we have no need for holy discontent. We settle into where society has situated us, at ease in the status quo. We lose our agency, urgency, and vision. Most of all, we lose our drive to bring love into the world; we concentrate on loving ourselves and all the people who are already "in."

Without holy discontent we settle for an insipid or apathetic existence. We are salt without saltiness. And like any mischievous woman, I desired to be a little saltier. I hadn't really forgotten who I was, but I had outgrown my former pastoral existence.

As much as Executive Jesus tempted me, I couldn't live in apathy, for that is not the kind of "discontent" that ushers in something new. Equally, Executive Jesus bade me to make myself smaller, but I refused to settle for the sacrilege of a small and mundane institutional existence.

Maybe that's why I landed in weddings, positioning myself in writing stories of love – the incredible ones, the romantic ones, and the ones that brought people back into the grasp of a loving God. I believe in the God of the impractical and impossible. And what is more impractical than standing with two people who are promising to love one another for the long and ambiguous future?

And I have seen it all – the unachievable and unworkable love stories. The unmanageable and unreasonable. I have witnessed the most ridiculous stories of love. Stories impossible to tell in staleness or without salt. I came to know (again) that my God is One of impossible love stories.

With this God becoming familiar again and calling me to what was possible (instead of telling me what was impossible), every moment became a little more holy. We're not meant to live in the mundane. I started to believe that for myself. It was a prayer of possibility, even for me.

Perhaps the prayer of possibility is also one that reminds us that learning to know Jesus doesn't happen all at once. It is not one moment but many moments of faith in which we learn the ways of Jesus. It is a story of love over a lifetime.

———

Once my men dressed in suits and argyle were done with their whirlwind photo tour of Paris, we made a final stop at the *Champ de Mars*. On a picnic blanket was the most stunning spread set for us – French butters and vegetables in every color of the rainbow. And just past the butter, set prominently in the center, was The Bread and The Cup. This couple's first married meal would be a feast of love.

I sat near the cup in between my new friends and served the meal I had served before. My black Converse sneakers had sassy pink ribbon shoelaces; I had ditched my heels by then. You can't follow love all over Paris in peep-toes.

The Iron Lady stood tall behind us. The sun warmed the lush green grass where tourists and locals alike sat to revere her greatness. She was tall and glorious, particularly when bathed in sunshine. The chill of the November morning was a distant memory, and we sat contentedly in our outdoor sanctuary.

Just as I had so many times before, I raised The Cup in my hands. I held it firmly between them, with veneration and ease. I had not forgotten. The bread of heaven and the cup of salvation given for two and for all. The sacred in the middle of the afternoon in a park. "This moment is holy." I pondered it all. Love was poured out, for two married folk and one pastor, plunged into possibility on a Tuesday in Paris.

Michelle Wahila

A Blessing for Becoming

Holy One, whisper quiet grace into my restless heart.
When fear clenches tight, loosen its grip with love.
Teach me to trust my unraveling.
I am becoming.

Wine and Boudoir in a Bathtub

THERE WAS THE IMPRESSION FROM THE PEW THAT THE PASTORS WERE ALL friends. There was laughter and there were smiles, so why not? No one knew that there was manipulation and forced smiles the rest of the time. Sundays were only a sliver of our lives.

We looked like friends on Sundays, but the week held our secrets. We lived and worked together – seven days out of seven. No Sabbath rest from the building that contained it all. All people saw were smiley friends on Sundays.

In theory, working and living together can bring community, and even joy. My situation could have brought a depth of human connection to Sundays. It could have sparked collaboration and creativity, or the daring vulnerability of friendship. Community is foundational to ministry, and this scenario could have given a sturdy foundation to the work of that place.

By its nature, ministry can be isolating. You must keep boundaries that mean parishioners are not friends. While colleagues can be, they don't have to be. It was a lonely existence in a foreign country, especially because the church was everything – employment, housing, and visa status. And it introduced me to the only other English speakers I knew.

Exiting the church doors meant leaving behind all the people. The ones you liked and the ones you knew didn't like you. Some were easier to let go of than others.

Goodbyes meant parting with the community, tenuous as it was. Starting over as a stranger in a strange land required more energy than I had to give. I had already given more of myself than I should have.

Isolation worked for a time. It's easy to contain a broken heart inside four apartment walls when the Paris mist dampens your clothes and your soul. When the skies began to turn blue again, and Paris began to wake from her winter slumber, I got restless enough to step outside my four walls.

I wasn't ready to "people" again, but I felt obligated to try. I figured that if I found a few folks with who I could grab a drink, explore Paris, or shove my face full of croissants, that it would be a win. Friendship wasn't a thought.

It happened rather organically. The wedding world in Paris is almost as small as the church world. We cross paths often. Unlike the forced church house friendships, these folks can choose you, and you them.

I was astonished by the wedding professionals. Their spirit of collaboration and creativity refreshed my tired existence. There was work, but also play. It was a welcome balance into which I was warmly invited by a community I didn't expect to find.

I couldn't figure out why anyone would want to befriend a broken-hearted pastor. I wasn't quite a creative, though I tried. I didn't exactly have a thriving business, though I hoped for one someday. I still spent numerous days trying to figure out where I had gone wrong in my last community – the church.

Even now, I felt broken; maybe, I was cracked open enough to let the light inside. If there was light, it was dull. The cracks rendered me defenseless to more heartache. And making friends felt like stark-naked vulnerability – exposing my heart.

Who needed friends anyway?

I never imagined that my spirit could be glued back together wearing lingerie in a bathtub with new friends. But here's to the unexpected dainty threadwork of communal joy.

I sifted through the black lace bras that were strewn about, covering my equally black leather loveseat. I picked up one delicate piece, gently rubbing the *dentelle* through my fingers. It was soft but edgy. I wanted to be both of those things.

I was shoving spicy lingerie, glitter confetti, black wine glasses, and sequined gowns into suitcases. It was nothing like packing granola, diapers, a laptop, and unread reports for long church days. My suitcase overflowed, but my heart more so.

I was off to a *manoir* in the Loire region of France for a weekend with wedding experts. It was an epic photoshoot weekend, created for people to experience boudoir for the first time. It had the intensity of Holy Week with less crucifixion, but just as much joyful anticipation.

The team was an incredible mix of professionals from different *métiers*. I was the amateur with a frilly vision. A wild vision at that.

It's hard to trust others when you've been micromanaged for so long. It's easier when you can't take photographs or construct a flower arch. I can barely put on my own eyeliner, so I knew I couldn't do makeup or hair. I was compelled into a moment of reliance on others that resembled the possibility of community.

Breaking the cycle of distrust weds you to freedom. I was wed to possibility. This weekend held the frills and thrills of change.

It was intense. There were enormous florals to be assembled, multiple rooms to be decorated, wardrobe changes, makeup and hair, and a rotation of photographers flowing in and out of the grand manor house's rooms made of stone. It was a blur of work, laughter, and walking around more naked than I was accustomed to.

The lace briefs barely covered my rear. They covered more than the fur I was wearing on top. The photographer directed me to the black clawfoot bathtub that matched my lace *derrière*. I wrangled myself in, carefully placing the frilly ribbon-tied boots I was wearing over the tub's edge.

"Give me a great big smile."

I did. I remembered how to smile. It only took an untamed plan overflowing with underwear and floral sprays.

After he snapped what must have been a thousand photos, the other two lingerie-clad *femmes* squished me into the center of the tub.

"I can't believe we all fit!" I chortled more loudly than necessary when smushed next to two people in a tub. We were all giggling.

I contorted my body to show off the boots he was photographing. The images were for another vendor, gracious enough to lend us her wares for the photoshoot. That's how it worked. The pros shared their talents and treasures to build one another up. It was a foreign world to me.

The gemstone ring that adorned my finger had to be photographed as well. I pressed my hand outward for the photographer, as delicately as I could manage. I was awkward, as usual. My awkwardness was tempered by the gorgeous things and people surrounding me.

I'm sure I was elbowing someone's bosom the entire time. It wasn't easy to keep my balance in a bathtub filled with friends. The smiles came easier than balance. It had been that way for so long.

"This is the first time that I've ever been in a tub filled with my friends, dressed in lingerie."

"Me too," I snickered and snorted.

"Cheers to that!"

We may have been near naked, but we were clothed in joy.

We toasted again. It was worth the second clink. "Cheers to friends!"

Indeed. Cheers to a community who shows up for you. Cheers to the ones who are there when you have an idea so wild that it ends in a clawfoot tub sprinkled with roses, covered in lace, and squished together. We lifted our black glasses heavenward; this toast was a joyful celebration of the people. I had come to call these people friends.

In the middle of a boudoir photoshoot, I had the audacity to find joy wrapped in friendship. It felt as foreign as the professional world in which I was now immersed. My heart was stripped bare inside the church. When I left that community behind, I knew that I never wanted to feel so bare again. It's risky to dip your toe into the tub if you think you might get burned. Community didn't feel quite worth the risk.

True community gives you a place to come as you are, even with a wounded heart. I dared to sit my almost bare *derrière* down in a bathtub; maybe, bare doesn't mean broken. Surrounded in laughter and delight, this community gave my vulnerable heart a place to rest.

Michelle Wahila

A Toasting Benediction

Raise your glass; there is joy in this room!
Blessed is the community that celebrates together.
We have opened our hearts to one another.
Blessed is the community that celebrates together.
Shared our sorrows and delights.
Blessed is the community that celebrates together.
In the vulnerability of authenticity there is hope.
Blessed is the community that celebrates together.
For this collective *clink,* we offer our gratitude.
Blessed is the community that celebrates together.
Raise your glass; there is joy in this room!
Here's to more!

Baby Chicken Blessing

I ROLLED OVER AND RELUCTANTLY SLID OUT OF BED, NOT BECAUSE I DID not want to wake, but because I was entirely relaxed – a feeling that I had forgotten existed for so long. I had to leave the comfort of my warm place and the black and white kitten paws kneading my arm. I am not a morning person. Thank God my Valiant Knight recognizes this well-known fact and preemptively brews a pot of coffee to lure me out of bed. I heard the dinging of the coffee pot and realized that it was time.

Unlike in times past, when I couldn't bear to drag myself out of the comfort (or safety) of my bed, today was different. My feet snuggled themselves into my fuzzy pink slippers, and I was off. I dropped a heaping pile of things I needed for the day into my work bag: rosé champagne and two glasses, my iPad, high heels, a red lipstick, tissues, and an enormous bouquet that had been reposing serenely out of my kitten's grasp on the balcony all night.

I snatched up my phone, kissed my boys, and was out the door. My silvery chrome sneakers hit the pavement, and I wondered if I would make the bus. Otherwise, I would have to make it by foot. It didn't matter; I was content walking. I looked around me, gazing up at the Eiffel Tower and breathed in the sweet scent of roses wafting up from the stunning bouquet in my hands. Full of joy and caffeine I was off to work.

Could I really call it work? To be honest, I wasn't sure. How ridiculous was this moment? I had a bottle of pink champagne rolling around my bag and it wasn't even ten in the morning. I checked on the glasses clinking around my leopard print purse and sifted through to find the small white plastic clerical collar piece that I was hoping I hadn't forgotten.

I made a list and checked it twice. I still had nervous butterflies every single time I went out the door. The good kind of butterflies. Like the ones that come with surprise parties and first kisses.

At the bottom of my leopard bag under the champagne bottle, I found that small plastic rectangle and fished it out of my purse. I finagled it into the collar of my dress, until it sat perfectly in between the two pieces of black lace flanking it.

As I was maneuvering the plastic piece into my collar, I looked up and saw an older woman staring at me. I had made the bus and slung my big bag on the seat next to me while I dealt with my collar. I simply smiled at her, thinking she probably had never seen a woman pastor on the bus making her way to an early morning wedding, wearing red lipstick and carrying champagne.

The sun was rising over *Trocadero* and the Eiffel Tower was perfectly illuminated with early morning sunbeams. They were the kind that could make your eyes sparkle in photographs and your soul sparkle in the moment. I was standing in the most beautiful city in the world preparing to do my job.

I still wasn't sure I remembered how to be a pastor. I was clunky and awkward. It wasn't unlike how I felt in the oversized pulpit in *that* place. I felt like I would fumble it all; please God don't let me drop the rings. I could see them rolling down the stairs of *Trocadero*.

I hadn't even met this couple. This was a favor for one of my friends. I was excited to officiate another wedding though because it had been a long time. In the place with the oversized pulpit, I was far too female for the privilege of officiating weddings.

Because I was still entangled in the definition of pastor *that* place had, still entrapped in the institutional within-the-building concept of weddings, I came to the moment before me feeling out of practice and out of courage. I had been leaning into my new role as a stay-at-home mom for the last year, trying to leave my pastoral identity behind me.

I was also learning to love myself again, without the role of traditional pastor tied to my worth. It was bizarre to stand before people who were seeking a pastor to speak love over them. I came without confidence and with emotions swirling. I allowed *the* Spirit to calm my spirit and leapt into the moment.

One favor for a friend – a single wedding, full of nerves and joy and a champagne toast afterwards. It was delightful, but more delightful was the tumbleweed of weddings that followed. With the requests and bookings came a new schedule: I often needed to rise early to get ready for morning weddings. It was a new rhythm to my life, for sure. I gave thanks for the pot of coffee brewed with love by my dearest spouse.

The scent alone would beckon me out of bed, even before my alarm would sound.

In addition to copious amounts of coffee I readied myself to appear in someone's wedding photos (like, for forever). There was even more lipstick and eyeliner in my life now. This new life came upon me so quickly I didn't even realize that I had traded my lady briefcase for extra eyeliner.

Equally, I readied myself for the holy moment that was going to take place. I started my mornings with a prayer of love, welcoming the Holy Spirit into what was going to happen throughout the day. I prayed for the couple, by name, and took time to reread the words written for them.

No longer a survival technique, coffee and prayer centered me. Weddings can feel rushed because of tight schedules, but if I started the day with my warm brew and blessing, I came with calm joy into the moment. It was a sacred start for a holy happening.

I was being called into the thrilling and creative chaos of someone's wedding day. Though it was quite possibly the most important day of someone's life, I never felt the pressure to perform, as I once did. I came with my leopard bag and a champagne toast to celebrate. And I came as myself, ready to participate in the joy and tears that the Spirit would bring. Not for one wedding or one hundred weddings was I asked to sacrifice my joy to please Executive Jesus.

I was readying myself for the day ahead. My Baby Chicken had snuck out of his room and into my bed at some point. I sort of knew he was there, but it was early, and I didn't want to disturb him. I continued my morning bathroom routine.

Baby Chicken was quiet, and I just let him be. I enjoyed the beautiful silence until Baby Chicken broke it with his high-pitched little voice. "Mommy, I read your message."

"You did?"

"Yes, the iPad was open to it."

"Ok, what did you think?"

"You have an important job, Mommy, speaking love."

"Yes, I sure do."

"You're lucky."

"I know, buddy. I am so so lucky and blessed."

My sensitive Baby Chicken sees more liminal space between heaven and earth than most people. I always count his thoughts as precious, not just because they are his, but because he has a way of grounding the spiritual in our earthly realities. With five-year-old words, in a squeaky voice, he spoke of things most adults don't understand.

To hear him recognize the responsibility, privilege and blessing of what I do now filled my heart. To see him interested in a couple, the message I have written for them, or even the simple details like the bouquet (he will occasionally pick them up with me from our local *fleuriste*), reminds me that the small things matter.

On a wedding day the minute details can make or break the day. I slipped the tiny plastic rectangle into my collar and claimed my calling. Small things can carry love into the world each day. It's a privilege to be a keeper of the sacred small.

My little Baby Chicken was watching me prepare for the day. I had my pearls, and champagne and a bouquet filled with delicate purple flowers resting near my leopard bag and the chrome Nikes that faithfully carry me as I galivant through Paris marrying people. He often watched me pack up for wedding days. Where he once begged me to stay, he now blesses me forward as I go. His sweet loving benediction "to marry my couples well" is my daily sending song. I don't leave home without it. I may fumble around, but I go with the power of the Holy Spirit and my Baby Chicken, into the world.

Somewhere along the way I traded the wrath of Executive Jesus for a new calling. With bouquets and glasses clinking around in the bottom of a leopard bag, I am the keeper of small things that make a wedding day complete in Paris. And I am charged to do this well: speak love.

Michelle Wahila

Baby Chicken's Benediction

Contributed by my Baby Chicken

May we accept joyful embrace
And share laughter together.
May we be considerate with one another
And generous with our smiles.
May we speak encouragement and compliments,
Never hesitating to share delight.

Kleenex for Happy Tears

I WAS STANDING AT THE CENTER OF A LONG BRIDGE WITH THE METRO LINE six rattling above me. Awaiting the most striking bride to walk down the aisle toward me, I had a momentary flashback. A year earlier my life was vacant of such an abundance of ruffles and roses. I remembered sitting in my apartment, quite content to be in my home, but discontented by the ministry I was missing.

That memory sparked a single glistening tear to roll down my cheek. It escaped; grief has a way of doing that. I may have been free, but the chains were still there. Some days my heart ached so much that I would just sit on my two-person loveseat alone, while the tears streamed.

I wouldn't even know how much time passed. I counted moments by tissue boxes and set an alarm to pick up Baby Chicken and Little Dragon from school. At least that moment contained more joy than grief.

Just as I allowed that flashback to float into my mind, I also allowed it out. I reoriented myself to the incredible moment that I was witnessing. It was a moment of pure joy, wrapped in love. The look on the bride's face made that evident, and a single crystal tear strolled down her cheek as well. Her bride approached.

I had a momentary sense of how "just right," this moment was, for the couple and for me. Like the bride standing next to me, and the one approaching, I was overwhelmed by the joy and the love contained in this moment.

I smiled a genuine smile. "This is the person I am," I thought. I had just buried her for so long that I had forgotten how she felt. Somehow, I just needed to cough up some dirt and get out of the grave.

I didn't miss the institution. I missed the people, the holy listening, and the liturgical elements of my life. I never thought of myself as overly religious but missing these things made me realize how churchy I was. I yearned for the old hymns that I knew by heart, for the changing of the liturgical colors and the cycles of church life.

All the crap I had sold myself over the years – that I was inadequate, not enough, and not at all capable – was lies that stole my true identity. The person smiling, ready to serve, and enfolded in joy and love was who I was. Maybe it was the Holy Spirit herself showing up, but I was overwhelmed.

It wasn't grief overwhelming this time. The grace of knowing my own identity rushed through my beating heart in real time. Had I been ruffled by some forgotten grace?

With gratitude for the moment, I accepted the gift of standing before this couple, serving them, and speaking love over their lives. This was pastoral privilege.

I almost turned it away. I still wasn't really working, and telling myself that was the way it should be. I was done with churchy things.

It was another dear pastor who sent the message, all the way from Pittsburgh to Paris. Two of her parishioners wanted to elope to Paris, but these ladies couldn't find anyone to officiate. Dang it, I had to do it.

I wanted to offer this pastoral care, even if I didn't want to be associated with the church. And it was nothing like a church call. I was deep in the details.

A photographer? Yes, I knew one. Champagne and glasses? I could do that. Remember to wear good walking shoes for Paris and change into your heels upon arrival. This pastoral care looked a lot like tending to the tiny, ruffled details of fascinators, vintage heels and an antique brooch.

It was most certainly not a call in a church. It was a cold and soul dampening November day in Paris. I was trekking to *Bir Haikim* bridge to do a small favor for a friend. I wasn't standing inside the grand stone sanctuary of the church or the oversized pulpit. I wasn't even sitting in the boardroom attempting to appease Executive Jesus.

I wasn't standing inside the church doors presiding over worship or sitting around the boardroom table moderating a meeting; I stood, very much outside, with the Paris mist to remind me with an unmistakable sense that this was a moment to which I had been called. It's hard to parse out calling, but had I seen a rainbow or chariot ablaze, I wouldn't have been shocked.

My heart was ablaze, and that made me certain enough. I stood under one of the most iconic bridges in all of Paris, with its antique chandeliers serving as witnesses, to marry two of the most incredible people I had ever met. The was rain, plenty of tears, and a toast.

I could only describe it as the most intangible of spaces. Heaven touched earth. Two people made their promises to love one another for eternity in the center of Paris in the rain. Soaked in cold November droplets and love, I think I may have heard Jesus calling my name, beckoning me to finally come out of the tomb. I stepped out, back into my calling, that wedding day.

I already knew what it felt like to think I was nothing but a failure. For several years there was a window where I failed well at all the things – pastor, wife, mother. Somehow those failures freed me. They allowed me to see calling as something different and maybe even separate from a call, in a particular church. On that November wedding day, I hadn't come with expectations. God showed up anyway.

Even if I had failed completely at this wild and holy calling, I was beginning to think that my past ties to Executive Jesus didn't matter. I thought there might be a greater story within me. Failures and all.

In the end, my failures freed me from the expectations I had of myself, of the institution, and of ministry. They freed me for more joyful expectation to infiltrate my heart and my work. The shackles were broken, as I admitted to myself that God's grace could show up – outside the church and even for me. I was disheveled and enamored by the truth of this grace.

———

As the couple kissed, the crowd that gathered around us clapped and cheered. The brides twirled in their dresses of head-to-toe ruffles and silk and waved pink bouquets victoriously in the air.

Love had won, and I was blessed to witness the victory. I stood, a little ruffled myself, smiling from ear to ear.

It was not the first wedding I had officiated, and it wasn't going to be my last. For the first time, in a long time, I felt free. I had more joy than questions, more passion than anger, and more hope than sorrow.

Somehow, standing in a crowd of people I didn't know, outside, performing a wedding, felt like church to me. It was churchier than anything inside the church doors had felt in a long while.

Maybe it was the romance of a city in which I forgot I was living. Maybe it was affirmation or a shove from the Holy Spirit.

There was something sacred in an eloping couple who drew a crowd of witness around them. People they didn't know, bystanders who stopped to see love, surrounded us. It was the most unexpected cloud of witnesses.

———

People are drawn to weddings. They are attracted to love and want to witness it. It's why we honk our car horns when we drive by a wedding, and why we stop to say congratulations to a newly married couple even when we don't know them. We want love to win.

We want to share in a story that says, "this is truth," and to hear it proclaimed again and again. A wedding is a visible reminder that love is concrete. We hear the "I do" and see the rings exchanged and there is hope in the promise of love being made.

It ushers us into something greater — if only but for a fleeting moment. Even skeptics can be swayed by a kiss when it's right there in front of them. If only for a few minutes on any given morning in Paris, where a crowd of unrelated souls gather because they see something bizarre, love reigns.

My pastoral heart tells me that this is a truth people want to hear over and over throughout their lives. It's part of what the true community of faith is called to do – to tell the story of love and to *be* that story. Weddings are simply one of life's transitional moments that happen to tell that story well. Life is full of liturgical moments meant for telling a love story.

We want to be gathered in, and to hear the ways in which we are a part of the story. We humans desire to love and be loved. Without a doubt, we want to know that we belong to love.

The beauty of a wedding – silk ties, cathedral veils, stunning bouquets – may draw our attention. The celebration invokes joy but the love we experience at a wedding captures our hearts the way only something bigger than ourselves can.

In John's gospel, Jesus' very first miracle just happened to be performed at a wedding. There he was, fully divine, hanging out at a wedding banquet. I appreciate a God who loves a good party!

The picture of the marriage banquet is throughout Scripture and is given as a picture of heaven. Jesus brought heaven to earth – our first glimpse of that was at that wedding in Cana. Water into a wine – a sign of more. There's abundance in the God who celebrates us and wraps us into a story of love.

Love is a story that moves us – sometimes to tears. I'm ready now, for those glistening droplets of saltwater. I come prepared in my black ballgown with pockets. From my perfectly hidden pocket I pull out a tiny white package for every couple.

The dainty Kleenex package is marked with flawless calligraphic letters, "For happy tears." I hold Kleenex in my pocket and stories of love. And these sacred things hold me too.

A Blessing of Tears

O Divine Spirit, capture my tears in your heart. Bring comfort to my sorrowful weeping. Accept my sobs of joy as an offering to your glory. Allow the water flowing forth from inside of me to nourish my soul and beget refreshment. Whether in bliss or with burden, embrace all of who I am in the depths of your love.

Re-formation and Resuscitation

STEPPING OUT MY DOOR WITH THE ABILITY TO BREATHE IN FREEDOM WAS A welcome change. I wasn't running to meetings or packing my bag for a fourteen-hour day. My shoulder bag was still packed full, nevertheless, I felt lighter.

I only had one bag, holstered over my shoulder, containing a tiny golden Eiffel Tower, a certificate with swirls and flourishes, a tiny container of bubbles, and champagne, of course. The clickity-click of my peep-toed black pumps on the cobblestone took me back to their clicking on the stairs that took me upward into the dark wooden and very mighty pulpit of Sundays past.

Same heels, different day, and different life.

I never imagined being revived by the holiness of the city that I had once struggled to consider home. Was it home? I couldn't be sure. Some days I felt like one of the tourists I would pass on my way to work, admiring the greatness of architecture and history surrounding me.

Once my peep-toed heels got me where I was going, and I stopped long enough to breathe deeply, I would look around at the passers-by and realize I was part of the city now too. Perhaps, I was not more than a sojourner here, and I would have but a moment in this gorgeous place. But if only a moment was granted to me, I was going to enjoy what was given.

The summer season made the city come to life with visitors. Tourists seemed to dance and twirl around me, snapping their selfies and pointing toward the majestic Eiffel Tower soaring in the background. Laughter filled the air. I shared this space with other pilgrims. I imagined we were all there for quite the same reasons – to experience beauty, to delve into joy, to reach for love. As my feet sunk a bit farther into the grass, I realized I belonged here in this moment.

I emerged from my pilgrim's dream when I heard someone calling my name from a distance. My eyes were drawn to the layers of ruffled lace trailing behind a gorgeous woman wearing a tiara. By her side was a well-suited man in dark glasses. They could have been straight out of the pages of Vogue. I glanced down at the bouquet of soft pink roses that I would soon hand off, to be held by the woman adorned in ruffles and lace.

They held hands as they approached the spot where I had settled myself. The gentleman wearing the green suit paused, and I could see that he was holding an arm full of frills and flounces, helping his bride step over the curb. He trailed behind her, ever so slightly, as she wove her way up the dirt path toward me. When they arrived, we both fluffed ruffles, and I handed her the bouquet of pink roses I was holding.

"Do you like them?"

"They are perfect!"

"So are you! Now, who is ready for a wedding?"

I had selected a spot in a little garden where you could see the Eiffel Tower peeking through treetops. It was as perfectly adorned with flowers as the ruffled bride. The three of us watched the ducks swimming in the small pond just right of us.

I held out my tiny Eiffel Tower and let them each drop rings onto her. "It's not every day that a tiny Eiffel Tower gets to hold your wedding rings in front of *the* Eiffel Tower."

"It's true," they agreed.

"But here we are!" I exclaimed.

There we were in the middle of the city. The couple said their vows as Lady Eiffel observed. The ducks waddled by as rings were exchanged and the crowd that had gathered clapped as newlyweds kissed.

"What a perfect moment!" And I encouraged them to stop and take it all in…

The sojourner's greatest gift is the experience of the moment that has brought them there. It's the end of one quest and the beginning of another adventure. It's every moment of the past that has paved the way, and it is the future that is found by the next courageous step forward.

In the intersection of what has brought us to a moment and what sends us forth to the next is the opportunity to simply *be*. When we find ourselves here, and we pause long enough to take it all in, we find the depth and breadth of what makes us human.

We find joy and sorrow. We weep, wail, and wonder. We giggle and raise our glasses, toasting to the moments. We are formed and reformed in the sacred present.

Every time I stepped out of my apartment door and back out into the city to do my job, I was formed and reformed in my present moment. The sacred present pulled me toward wholeness. I was resuscitated with cufflinks, organza, and love day by day.

After the ruffled bride signed her name to the wedding certificate covered in calligraphic flourishes, I reached into my leopard bag and pulled out a paper *cornet* filled with dried rose petals and biodegradable glitter. This couple, like so many who come to elope, were far from home and their family and friends.

Everyone's reasons are different; I honor them all. And I know what it's like to be far from home. I cannot be family and friends, but I can be a pilgrim alongside of two, in a place where lovers from every corner of the world come to live their own moment of passion.

For every moment that once passed when I wished I could bottle joy and stick it into my purse, I now grabbed joy from within it. The paper cone contained rose-scented glittered joy for a couple who didn't think they would have a grand exit because their family and friends were too far away. A grand exit created in love – I once had a moment that I thought would be the same.

I placed them in the middle of where the Eiffel Tower was looking over our ceremony spot, giving instructions so the photographer could capture the moment transforming it into a memory.

"Put the book-ette in the hair!"

"Ummmm, what are you saying?" I was starting to giggle because I was certain I was a victim of his French accent. Sometimes his accent was thick enough that even I was confused.

"Oh! The bouquet in the air! Put your bouquet in the air!" I got it, finally. We laughed all together.

With pink roses facing heavenward, the newlyweds glided toward us. I took a handful of glittered joy and tossed it in the air. Surely our joy would reach heaven. Little petals showered the two of them, and they stopped to sneak a kiss. Another sacred moment glittered with joy.

I glanced over at the photographer, who had been snapping away. He was smiling too. If Lady Eiffel could have clapped, she would have. The crowd, still gathered, cheered. "Very Married!" I proclaimed. Two summer sojourners claimed their joy in Paris. There was no place I wanted to be more than in that moment.

A Sojourner's Prayer

Come. Holy Spirit,
Bring what you will.
Rustle, rumble and refresh
My soul.
Pull, prod, and place me
In the path that leads toward abundance.
Though I feel voiceless,
You bring breath
That allows me to experience anew
Your presence
Along the way.
Though I may be wandering,
You call me toward the wholeness of home.
Compel me toward love on this path –
The winding trail of this moment.
Bring what you will.
Come, Holy Spirit.

Fireflies and Glowworms

SUMMER EVENINGS WERE SOME OF MY FONDEST CHILDHOOD MEMORIES. WE played through the day until dusk, riding two-wheeled bikes with pink streamers coming out of the handlebars and hopping between all the neighborhood houses until it was time to go home. The long summer days were a never-ending vacation dream. But when the fireflies began to come out, another perfect day of childhood leisure would draw to a close.

Sometimes we wouldn't end up at our own home, but that of a neighbor. Every house in the neighborhood felt like home. We would ask to call our parents as to not worry them. Someone would dial our number and then stretch out the long plastic cord, handing us the phone out the door, "Can I stay a little longer, pretty please?" and summer days would transform into summer evenings.

As dusk turned to twilight, the fluorescent green glow of fireflies would emerge out of nothing. Their entrance was the true essence of summer nights. We followed them with glass mason jars and nets, hoping to capture the tiny glowing lights and keep the brilliance of summer glowing forever.

We ran in circles, following the glowing dots, admiring the way they defied nature to light the way in the dark. If we were lucky

179

enough to catch a lime green beauty, we would hold the tiny sacred light of summer in our hands for as long as it would stay. If it stayed long enough, we might drop him into a jar – not forever, just enough time to appreciate his perfect light.

We would release him back to the summer night, where he joined the others to glitter twilight with glowing green. They zipped around the sky, making us dance in circles to follow their radiance. We danced in the brightness of sky glitter until our parents called us home.

I wanted my own children to have the leisure of summer nights the way my spouse and I did. Paris didn't exactly provide for that. Although occasionally we would play in the *Champ de Mars* until the sun went down and the rats came out. But the long trek home from the park to home would do me in…

The school bags, stroller, and snack bags weighted us down; it was the longest kilometer ever. There were almost always tears because we were hangry. When we finally crossed the threshold of our forty-two square meters, we would drop the bags in the doorway and slump onto the floor.

Living in Paris meant living in the extremes of being struck by beauty and slumping on the floor. Paris was stunning in architecture, culture, and cuisine. But city life was exhausting.

From the market to the metro, everything took effort. Playing in the park was no exception. By the time we reached home, we could only slump.

I hoped for more than lumps of slump for my kids. Though Paris gave us myriad opportunities, as the boys grew, we needed more space, fewer video games, and fresher air. Summers in New York provided a good dose of fresh air and nostalgia. And once we moved to the countryside, our nostalgia became reality.

The summer days that came with our house in the French countryside melted into warm summer nights that invited us to stay outdoors until stars lit up the sky. The evenings were occupied with the right amounts of work and play. The buzzing of the lawnmower in the West Orchard didn't drown out the laughter of boys on bikes.

The boys rode their mountain bikes through the edges of my flower garden, testing their brakes on my poppies. At the edge of our concrete sidewalk, there was a mound of dirt that did not exist the day before. It was at least a dozen wheelbarrows full of garden dirt. It had been patted down with shovels and watered to keep its shape. A mountain bike jump was born that day.

The last jump and twilight came simultaneously. The day's creation of dirt had to rest until the light came back again. The lawnmower's headlights lit up a path from the farthest orchard, and my Valiant Knight came to join us on the patio, where my two dirt covered boys had joined me.

My three guys cracked open cans of root beer; I had been hiding them for just such an occasion. They were imported from Grandma's house in New York in almost oversized suitcases. The warmth of a summer's evening deserved the joy of root beer. For myself, a cold can of cream soda... It was the American dream of vanilla bliss. I too, cracked open my can.

We toasted with cans that reminded us of all the goodness of summer. New York met France with the taste of home. "Cheers!" we all declared. And we chugged the flavor of a midsummer night's dream.

After the sweetness of summer-in-a-can was finished, we noticed the first of the evening's stars twinkling above us. It was late by now, past ten o'clock. The first star lit the way for the others, and we gazed upon a sky filled with tiny lights. It was as dizzying as it was beautiful.

To stay awake in the hope of catching a glimpse of shooting star tails later, I wiggled around in my Adirondack chair. It was past my bedtime, but summer nights always bid you to stay. As I was shifting my weight to get comfortable, I caught a hint of glowing green across the lawn. "Look boys! Fireflies, just like at Grandma's!"

Both boys jumped to their feet to investigate the tiny bright lights. From the patio it was hard to make out exactly where the glowing lights were. Once the kids descended onto the lush grass of summer, I realized they had planted themselves on the lawn.

Both were kneeling, and Baby Chicken yelled to us from across the grass, "They aren't fireflies!"

"What do you mean?" I didn't quite understand because I could see the fluorescent green in their hands.

"Come!" Little Dragon invited me down to join him in summer's lush sanctuary. Reluctantly, I peeled myself out of my wooden resting place to meet the children on their knees.

"Glowworms!" I exclaimed. "These are glowworms." I didn't even know they were real. So much of existence still felt unreal.

The grass was aglow, glittered with fluorescent dots. Baby Chicken was holding one darling on the side of his hand. Its glowing backside wiggled slightly, and we giggled at the thought of a fairytale insect on our lawn.

I imagined the Creator fashioning these little creatures to place delicately among the blades of grass. Unnoticeable by day, now they put on an incredible lightshow that matched the stars above us. Their story was bright, punctuating the darkness of night with their very existence.

I was taken aback by this mystical little worm who was glittering our grass with light. I wondered why I hadn't noticed them before. Conceivably, I had been too busy or too tired. Maybe I just hadn't sat in the darkness long enough. Though I had been there plenty.

I wanted to notice the light. If it meant slowing down, doing less, or doing nothing but being still, I wanted to capture the feeling of fluorescent-green-light-joy. I remembered; I held it in a mason jar as a child. My children held it in their hands on a summer night too. It was, perhaps, the feeling of ease that came with summer.

It was the glittering existence of something so small that was like a creative ode to joy. Why did this little light exist here? I wondered if my little glowworm friend knew his purpose; I was still trying to figure out mine.

As I watched the little green light glowing with a pulsing rhythm that I imagined to be a heartbeat, I was overwhelmed by the way he was both miniature and brilliant. He was perfect.

I held the creative imagination of the God who made me in my hands. Wonder abounded. I hadn't felt so awe-inspired in such a long while.

I thought I had lost my imagination. I left behind energy, intelligence, and maybe even love at the church doors already. Those words pulsed in my mind: energy, intelligence, imagination, love. The words of my ordination vows. I spoke them in front of God, family and friends, to proclaim the way I serve as pastor.

Those words throbbed through my core, more quickly than the bright light pulsed in my hand. Determined not to lose this part of who I was, I grasped that little light and prayed. I held onto the light of hope; it was there in wiggly lime perfection in the palm of my hand.

That prayer was the way forward and maybe the way home. One summer night, I tiptoed into wonder; it was a season of reimagining, reorienting, and reestablishing who I was in the light of the Divine. I just needed a bit of fluorescent glitter and some creative imagination to light my way.

Michelle Wahila

The Prayer of a Spark

It's dark here, inside my head.
Bleak and meager, dimness spread.
My spark has disappeared.
I'm not sure I can find my way.
My little spark is dampened – The one I have betrayed.
I used to shine of stardust, but I'm a dusty shade of grey.
I don't think I'm meant for darkness; I'm much too dull this way.
I'd like the light of vibrancy to come and light my path.
I wish to carry light again; it made me weep and laugh.
It is a spark that makes me very *me*, like the shining stars above.
So, glitter my life with light divine, gush over me with love.
Sprinkle me with inspiration, so my brightness will return.
Surge through me with encouragement, that my little spark would
burn.

The Courage of Garlic and Potatoes

WE MOVED TO THE FARMHOUSE IN THE SUMMER, THE SAME SEASON THAT had seen us move to Paris. We had many fewer boxes this time, and two extra cats. We packed ourselves too, every precious Paris memory into boxes destined for the countryside. Instead of waiting for our things to arrive on the other side of an ocean, we loaded our new to us car (the first one we had owned in a decade), filling it to almost over-flowing. Each weekend before the final move out of Paris, the ritual of Tetris-like car packing pulled us toward our new French life in the countryside.

Once our first autumn passed; we braced for winter. The darkest months of winter in the countryside, however, are nothing like the darkness of Paris winter. In Paris, we hibernated, to avoid as much as possible having to brave the penetrating mist. There's darkness, cold and mist in the countryside as well, but there's always work to do – even in winter. Hibernating is not a viable option.

We need wood to heat our nineteenth-century farmhouse. Moving, sorting, and chopping is work for my Valiant Knight, who never expected to be wearing red and black checked buffalo plaid while felling trees when we moved to Paris all those years ago. But, *voilà*, he had traded his former kingdom of the commute for one of the *bûcheron*

Michelle Wahila

(lumberjack) that now keeps our family warm through woodchopping and love.

My work is to keep the family fed; I am the keeper of the *potager* (vegetable garden). I had not kept a garden since moving from Pittsburgh, and worried that I'd forgotten what to do – like so much of the expertise I had in my former life. But with every season, the garden work went from distant memory to the present tense.

It was the doing that brought the knowing back. Putting my hands into the dirt reminded me what to do – the tilling and tending, the weeding and working the soil. I surrounded myself with rakes and spades and vegetables in rows, singing quietly while I toiled in the hope of a harvest. The garden gave me a voice that I didn't have in meetings. I found more hope in the dirt than the pulpit.

Planting winter vegetables requires the most courage and toughest labor. Turning heavy waterlogged clay soil tired my body but not my spirit. I lifted the dense topsoil with my spade out of the trench where the garlic would rest for the winter.

My feet sunk down into the wet earth, grounding me. The straight lines prepared for garlic trenches stood out in a mostly bare garden. The summer harvest season was done now. I wiggled my feet free from the mud and reached for the garlic heads that would soon reside in the trenches I'd just dug. In my hands I held what was left of last year's garlic harvest.

It was the memory of our first full growing season held in my palms. The last of the previous harvest would become the seed of the next. Little garlic gems would rest in the frosty ground through winter and awaken in the spring. One year gave birth to the next, stirring life into what were otherwise the bleakest days of winter.

"Courage, little ones!" It was a simple prayer for sleepy winter cloves.

I gently pulled apart each head and popped the tiny garlic gems into the ground. I covered them with the muddy red clay soil I had moved from the trenches. So much happens in the trenches. But for now, they were hunkered down to wait.

Potatoes are the other favorite of winter that reside in a trench. The previous owners of our farmhouse (the French grandparents we inherited with the purchase of the farm) left us with hundreds of potatoes that offered plenty of French fries for our first summer of grilling. They provided for us in potatoes and carrots; it was a gift of hope for the future of their home. For forty years they tended the land that they now entrusted to us. Potatoes were our homecoming.

To carry on their fried potato tradition, rows and rows of potatoes go into the ground every year. They must take a long winter's nap; so, they must go in early. The ground is still hard, but the trenches are dug deep because little potatoes rest their eyes far below the surface. Down into the trenches they go.

When spring wakes the potatoes from their slumber, petite green leaves sprout from the earth in less than straight lines. It's not time for them to wake, and we "hill them up," letting them rest a little longer. White flowers eventually adorn green leafy tops. They stay for a while, then fade away.

When the flowers fade and the leaves fall, it is time. The excavating of potato trenches is demanding but the digging of potatoes is delicate. The once slumbering tubers infiltrate outward; the trenches aren't so defined by the time they are ready to come out of the earth. The only way to dig potatoes is on your knees.

I traded my large spade for a handheld one and set out to collect my joyous collection of carbs. I entered the garden with a wooden crate full of nothing but hope. Soon, hopefully, it would be full of potatoes.

I took my foam kneeler to the trenches and placed it at the edge of brown potato tops. I kneeled at the altar of the hopeful harvest and started to dig. I took a rather uneducated guess at where I should place my spade.

The potatoes are tricky; I never quite figure them out. Have they grown sideways? Or down farther into the ground? Growth isn't always linear.

If you're overzealous with the spade, you'll damage the potatoes by guessing incorrectly where they have slept all winter. It's why the full-sized spade is not the right tool for the job. It requires something less obvious. You can't just bash through the soil expecting to find what you're looking for there...

Instead, I am on my knees. I unearth the earth-apples with the fervor of an archeologist uncovering a lost treasure from the ground. It's messy work that brings excitement of past hope squarely to the present.

I soon laid my hand-held spade aside, digging through with my hands. There were too many tiny tots to risk the spade. As I plucked them from the earth, I held up each spud examining their divots and fine skin. I wondered if their eyes could admire me the way I admired them. I dug down farther and wider making sure I hadn't missed any tiny outliers.

My hands and knees were covered in the dirt, but I wasn't bothered by the messy work. I placed even the tiniest of tots into the wooden crate. They belonged there too.

Life on my knees was not the same as it had been within the confines of the grey stone walls of church. It was just as messy, but more grounded. I came out of the garden dirty, but content. The garlic and potatoes gave me courage to continue. There was hope in dirt and the bleakness of winter.

A Messy Prayer

O Divine Creator, you have placed me within the splendor of your handiwork. Root me in thankfulness for this life. And though life comes with the bitterness and joy of every season, remind me that you are present in them all. Give me the courage to trust that life can spring forth from the darkness of winter. Give me the bravery to work in the trenches, that I would not shy away from the work necessary to grow. Ground me in love and press into my hands the strength to work through all the messiness that this life brings.

Breath, Grief, and Spring

My church time at *that* place felt like the longest Lent on record. My life felt "on hold" and captive to the institutional rules and the disdain of Executive Jesus. It was a dark tomb and dry bones without the promise of resurrection. It was always Lent and never Easter.

I spent so long in fight or flight mode that I was unaware how brittle I had become. I was thrust into what my body knew was a threat to my existence, over and over, and its imprint was all over my body. I couldn't avoid my declining health and rising anxiety, or how very out of breath I was. I couldn't ignore how dark life had become.

My heart was pulled toward the darkness of the holy night and the tomb. The heavy burden of being the institution's token female, and pain my family experienced in *that* place, were dark. I dearly wanted to exhale. With a sigh of deep relief, I wanted so badly to breathe in freedom, new life, and abundant love, pushing out of my core all the ugliness I had seen. After all, wasn't that the point of faith?

Before I could breathe in my new life, I had to sit with my old one. I had to honor those dry bones that had been swallowed up by the dust and decay of a broken institution and unwavering patriarchy. I had to fully see the damage that had been done in Jesus' name.

I had to look at my own scars and see the resurrection life, but I hadn't been dry bones for five minutes; resurrection was going to take me more than three days. When you spend years, not hours, minutes, or seconds in fight or flight, it takes the brain time to unravel what was. Before I could emerge from the tomb and shake off the grime, I had to honor the parts of me that had been placed there. The darkness had to be honored.

It was all a blur. I had held my breath and persistently spent time convincing myself – with confirmation by Executive Jesus – that I was wrong about everything. I sat in a dark place, until I was forced to flee.

I needed to be far enough away and safe enough before I could begin to process the pain. I had to convince myself that my body was safe enough to come out of the tomb. My heart wasn't sure it was ready to leave this darkest winter.

My bones had been dead and dry for a long time.

Springtime at La Fauvelière is a reawakening, and the first one spent on the farm brought me back from the dark valley where I had made my home. Daffodils will spring up from the earth well before the air feels spring enough. The tulips follow the daffodils, and the hyacinths fall in line soon after. But the reemergence of the birds is the most remarkable change.

The birds usher winter toward spring, like the coming of dawn. Well before sunrise one day, the birds begin their song again, carrying night into day in the space between winter and spring.

We hear the chirping even before the daffodils peek out of the ground. They are the prelude of changing seasons on the farm. Once this song starts you can be sure that the seasons are shifting. There's something "just right" about the way this time holds winter and spring in tension. It's already, but not yet…

Spring brings birdsongs, flowers, and a breadth of fresh work to farm life. We, too, awaken from winter's grip, like the birds. The labor of the homestead shifts from inside to outside, beckoning us back out into creation. The not-yet-warm breeze fills our nostrils with a newness that hasn't existed in a long while.

On one of the days I'd awakened to birdsong, I emerged from my stone house with clippers in hand. Readying myself, I launched into a new day and the necessary garden cleanup. My clippers were as rusty as I was.

Nevertheless, my clippers had their work cut out for them. They needed to meet the lavender in the front gardens and get reacquainted with the roses they hadn't seen since the autumn. The raspberries needed to be cut back to a perfect meter tall. The snipping and snapping of brittle branches pruned away winter to prepare for spring. Each season brought something to the next. I honored the work of winter, even as I trimmed it to make way for spring. She was waking up, and she was glorious.

I hadn't even made it halfway through the roses when I rested the clippers by my side, pausing my spring cleanup. Standing motionless, I inhaled deeply. The air was fresh and crisp. It smelled damp, but unmistakably like the newness of Eastertide. There was new life in every corner of the farm. Small wildflowers were popping up from the lush green grass covering the field. The crocuses danced about in the chilly breeze. The farm was coming back to life.

Regripping my clippers with the attention they deserved, I began trimming the roses again. Soon enough they would explode into pastel shades of pink, peach and yellow. The birds ushered in spring with their songs, the summer roses brought color to our lives.

From the first moments of divine creation, the Spirit has been the breath of life for all creatures. *Ruach* – breath – spirit. Breath fills us with life and draws us forward.

Grief, on the other hand, has a way of holding us in place. It had been the clenching in my stomach; the tears that fell without warning, making me unable to breathe; the nightmares; a severe degeneration of my joints; frequent migraines. Grief was the sinking feeling that lowered me into the pit.

Grief and breath. The two sat in constant tension within me. I both struggled to catch my breath and found breath to calm my racing heart. Every gasp was an invitation for the Holy Spirit to come resuscitate my dry bones. It was equally a remembering of the pain that had passed.

The tension honored the story I held inside. Grief honored the scars. Breath honored the life still within me.

With each inhale, I prayed for a re-creation. With every exhale my life's painful midnight ticked toward dawn. In my lungs' expansions and contractions, there was space to feel the grief and trauma that had held my body captive for a season. No matter how rusty I felt in prayer or purpose, breath created a place for God.

Making a space where grief and breath could sing together reminded me there was nothing I could feel that would frighten the Spirit's presence away. Her life-giving presence was as close as breath itself.

I finally exhaled entirely, with a breath deeper and wider than I thought possible. I was certain I heard the faint heavenly chirping of a birdsong. I was lighter now.

A Prayer of Light & Breath

If you have a candle, you are welcome to light it during this prayer as a visual symbol.

We will light this candle to remember the stories of our faith. In faith we are given the gifts of light, and breath, and hope. God offers to us and fills us with these precious gifts... over and over again.

Before there was anything, there was the faithful One who breathed breath over the waters to create. Out of the chaos of darkness came light, and it was good.

We remember that the LORD went before Israel by day in a pillar of cloud to lead them along the way, and by night in a pillar of fire to give them light, that they might travel by day and by night, guiding them faithfully on their journey.

We remember that the Son of Man breathed the breath of new life into dead bones, because even when all seems lost, there is hope.

We remember the light given to us in stories of Hanukkah and of Christmas, stories of abandonment, insecurity, and humbleness, that began one in a time of war, the other in a poor stable.

We remember that the loving God who kept the light shining in the temple and who came to share this life with us promises us comfort and peace. We remember too, that with faith must come perseverance.

Though we may not understand where our own stories fit into the stories of faith, we hold onto the stories we have been told.

[Lighting of the Candle]

As we light this candle, we give thanks for the communion of saints.

Michelle Wahila

Our stories are a part of a greater story. We are but one little light, in a sea of light.

As we cry out, we know that other faithful saints have cried out to you, O Lord. All of our laments are heard. Therefore, let us follow in these footsteps of the faith story coming to you with all of our heartaches, our sorrows, and the grief we have in this moment.

We watch the flickering little light. As it dances, we allow our thoughts to both come and go. If difficult parts of our stories seem to remain for a while, we let them linger, but then we take a deep, restorative breath.

[*Silence*]

The Lord knows our whole story. We are seen. We are known. The Spirit of God has made us; the breath of the Almighty gives us life.

We breathe in this story. We breathe in life.

The Roses of La Fauvelière

TODAY WAS THE DAY. THE FIRST WEDDING AT OUR HOME; OUR FARM, LA Fauvelière. I had waited and dreamt of this moment. I could have rested in that daydream forever, but there was work to be done. Grabbing my clippers from their kitchen home, I opened our Dutch door and headed outside.

Before I reached the rose garden, I caught myself in a moment of motionlessness. I had tilted my head upward toward the sky. It was a powdery blue hue that reminded me of the apartment walls that once held me hostage. Today there were no walls.

My gaze went back to the house. Above the doorframe was an Epiphany blessing written in chalk: 20 + C + M + B + 21. Clippers half-raised, my mind went back to the day we'd inscribed it. We received the keys to our new home in March. That was long past Epiphany, but there we were, standing outside our new home with a piece of chalk and a dinner bell, eager for blessing and with a new home waiting to be blessed.

My Valiant Knight had climbed a ladder to mark the doorframe in white-chalked hope. The year, plus the initials that came with the tradition of the Magi following the star to Bethlehem. Our pathway home was not perhaps as risky and circuitous as that of the Magi, but just as guided by the light of the Divine. The chalk blessing printed above the doorway would lead and remind us.

After the blessing that resembled an equation was placed above the door, my youngest reached for the brass dinner bell imprinted with "La Fauvelière" on its side. It was a gift from the previous owners and a piece of history meant to reside on the farm. The bell was at the heart of this place and Little Dragon rang it with all of his. It was an Epiphany blessing bright enough for March.

For a moment, I thought I could hear a little voice chanting, "I'm a dragon; I'm a draaaa-gon!" It was a distant memory and a reminder of the quick passage of time. My youngest was a big boy now, entering Junior High in the fall. He was old enough to see the beauty of a fresh start in a new home where he could ride his bike with the speed of his dragon spirit and be free.

We had looked at manors and castles and farmhouses galore. They were abundant, and it wasn't evident what life would be like outside of the city. It seemed grand, of course. Moving from the bustle of Paris to the fresh air and quiet of the countryside felt like a dream.

But we were still foreigners who knew nothing of living in rural France. We were lucky though. La Fauvelière came with the unexpected gift of French grandparents who helped light the way to abundant life in the countryside.

They told everyone that the Americans were coming to live in the home they had perseveringly rebuilt stone by stone. Merely a shell of history when they purchased it, they labored with love to restore La Fauvelière over forty years. We reaped the benefits of their time and their love.

Some days I still wonder if I will enter the kitchen to see a grey-haired woman stirring jam in a copper pot. When my Valiant Knight enters in his waders and sage-green zipper vest, I am sure it is *Monsieur*. Their imprint will always be here, in this place, with us. And sometimes their little red car brings them for a visit.

I came back to the reason I was standing there: we were expecting visitors, but not the little red car. Time was ticking before the bride, the groom and their family would arrive to our home.

There were not yet centerpieces for the table dressed in pink linen, nor a bouquet for our bride to carry. Off to the rose garden I went.

I plunged my nose into lemony-yellow petals to ensure that their intoxicating citrus scent filled my nostrils. Soft velvety edges tickled my cheek. I managed to immerse myself in the bloom I was trying to pick. She beckoned me – I obliged.

After removing my nose from her center, I admired her more wholly. Her shape was voluptuous, revealing an open center that was slightly more golden than lemon. Yes, she would do.

As I held her lightly, I reached for my weathered shears. Brushing against her thorny side startled me into the present; I must have been elsewhere. "Ouch! You're gorgeous and feisty." She was the dream.

After gently clipping her, I twisted her back and forth between my thumb and index finger. I was engrossed in the circular motion. Her twirls resembled a dance so dramatic that you could occasionally catch a glimpse of a ruffled petticoat. She was just as mysterious as any lace undergarment.

"You're the first today." It was a fact, simply stated. "Twelve more to go." Thirteen. It was always thirteen, never twelve. I don't believe in superstition, but I believe in creative balance.

Twelve more times I plunged, admired, clipped, and twirled. It was both ritual and a petition for what each beauty would become. One by one, every addition was gathered into the bundle. I tightly held those gathered with my gloved hand. The leather was filthy, and I could see the understated dusty-pink glove peering out from underneath. The dirty mauve disrupted my gaze, but only for an instant.

With my thirteen newly plucked beauties, I glided toward the west garden away from the *roseraie*. What more do you give to velvety-soft, citrus-scented beauties? Their companions must be subtle enough to complement curves but strong enough to sit firmly against the intensity of splendor.

The west garden is more rustic than perfect – a work in progress that is a compliment to the southerly facing prim and proper *roseraie*. The sweet aroma of thyme caught me by surprise as I entered. I must have brushed against her as I tiptoed through the herbs.

I tiptoed so as to not disturb the beauty of the garden. My movement was more a dance than a shrinking away. It was gentle rather than forlorn like it used to be.

The carrot tops waved a morning greeting as I glanced toward the rows of raised beds. "I'll get to you later, darlings."

How does one choose a complement to perfection? I knelt, as if in prayer, squarely inside the bed's border, squishing my knees into slightly damp soil. The sidewalk met the garden bed, but I preferred the soul of the soil to that of the path that had led me there. I was in the garden closest to vegetables and farthest from the roses now.

I slid off my mauve gloves so that I could run my fingers through the blue-green leaves capturing my attention. I plucked a leaf and popped it into my mouth. The sensation was crisp and cool.

My nose tingled. I deeply inhaled the joy of refreshment. "You are the perfect complement to perfection."

As I trimmed, a sweet scent rose like incense swirling through a cathedral. I hummed a selection of Symphony No. 9. My knees were covered in mud, but the dirt only served to ground me further into my labor. I returned my focus to the earth.

Before kneeling, I had tenderly placed all thirteen of my recently acquired beauties beside me while I gathered their companions. From the bed's edge, I glanced at my yellow enchantresses, noting how perfectly still they sat. Ready for their portraits, posing so effortlessly. They were going to be the perfect pair.

With the wild minty herbs in my left hand, I juggled my rusty shears and lemon beauties in the right. The beauty is becoming... "Are you ready? Shall we dress you?" I needed to get to it because our guests would be arriving soon.

There was a snip and a tuck and tendrils of satin ribbons. The perfumed blossoms and their green companions were adorned in satin, adding to their magnificence. I hoped our visitors would think they were beautiful too.

I took the last twirl before I gave her into the arms of another. The once single lemony wonder that had captured my intrigue blossomed. Now she exists not simply as beauty, but alongside others weaving together a tale of delight. Aren't the very best tales woven in this way?

Though we may not anticipate all the messy details of being plunged, admired, clipped, or twirled into a moment of life-giving joy, maybe we must rest in knowing that we deserve it. We are fully capable and worthy of carrying beauty. The simplicity of a velvety-soft touch adorned with cool refreshment invited me to recognize the freedom in this sacred truth.

Michelle Wahila

An Epiphany Blessing

This prayer can be said on Epiphany as a chalk blessing written over the door-frame of your home: 20 + C + M + B + the current year's ending. If the year is 2025, the first part of the year that is 20 begins the blessing and the last two digits end the blessing, 25. It would look like this: 20 + C + M + B + 25. The blessing can be concluded with a ringing of a bell, singing, cheering or clapping.

Bless this home, and your people here. Grant us an abundance of laughter. Fill these walls with joy. In all our comings and goings wrap us safely in your comfort.

It is said that Jesus made a home among people. Remind us to care for those without a place to call home. Never allow our family to forget that we are called to welcome the stranger – for hospitality reflects faith.

Above all, let all who enter here feel love, that together we would build a home of peace and welcome. Amen.

Summer's Crepuscule

SUMMER IS WEDDING SEASON'S ANSWER TO THE BUSYNESS OF EASTER, with fewer peanut butter eggs and more raspberries. If I am not in the raspberry patch, I am on a train traveling to or from a wedding, or I am standing along the Seine, gazing at the Eiffel Tower, performing a wedding. It is go-go-go, but also it is not.

June's long days have a way of making time for work and leisure. There's always work to be done – in the gardens, for school, in the kitchen, for my couples. I could busy myself, but I didn't have to… It wasn't a feeling with which I was yet comfortable.

The boys were still in school, but even with the demands of Junior High, we found ways to ease ourselves into the rhythms of summer. The warm almost summer breeze kept us outside after dinner, long enough to enjoy each other's company before the homework routine began.

The gardens invited us to stay a little longer. Red poppies danced in the gentle wind. Behind them the daylilies were in full bloom. The burgundy blossoms stood tall, peeking over the violet columbine.

It reminded me of my Pittsburgh lily. Our Pittsburgh urban oasis would have fit entirely into one corner of our farmhouse gardens. I beamed as I remembered the patch of grass that became a plentiful garden in the middle of the city. I sat comfortably in my oversized wooden throne gazing toward our willow trees, fully immersed in thoughts of how abundant life had become.

The little boys (not so little anymore) sat just ahead of me in two wooden Adirondack chairs. Cans of A&W root beer rested on the arms of their timber seats. They were the last cans of the previous year's trip to America. We knew it was time to go "home" to NY when we ran out of root beer. Summer was close; we would be going "home" soon.

To my right was my bearded Valiant Knight, dressed in buffalo plaid and sipping a glass of pink champagne. Our Muskoka chairs were close enough that we could hold hands; instead, we clinked glasses and sipped. The only sounds we heard were a distant cuckoo and laughter from the boys positioned ahead of us.

We were all facing the pond, tracking the "chicken ducks" (*poule d'eau*) zipping back and forth from edge to edge of the water. All four of us were content with chicken duck watching. Our contentedness stretched to dusk, which came much later now that it was June.

We stirred, knowing we must move onto the next thing – homework, dishes, and preparations for the next day of work. The color-changing sky held us in our contentment a bit longer. We were all looking up, as if looking for God, admiring her handiwork and the clouds resting on the horizon.

"Wow!" Little Dragon exclaimed in appreciation for the lightshow.

Wow, indeed. It felt like a dream. This quiet life, far from the bustle of the Paris city center was not the dream we had for our family a decade ago. It was the present though; fuller than any dream we could have imagined. In four timbered chairs, by the water's edge, an almost summer sunset beckoned us home.

Home had been NY, Pittsburgh, and Paris. Surrounded by flowers, our family was home once more. The other places always called to us, welcoming us when we stopped in to visit. In this moment, home was a stone farmhouse overlooking a pond with dancing willow trees surrounding us.

The planting and building of a new life together rooted us there. The picture of the move that brought us there was no less chaotic than the last move – carboard boxes containing memories of what had been, squeezed into our car between kittens and kids. It was the tired unstacking of boxes, anticipation, and hope. Some moves you pay for your whole life; others bring you a new one.

We packed, unpacked, drove, and then repacked our latte-colored SUV more times than I thought possible. How could forty-two square meters contain so much stuff? After moving from the church, our considerably downsized apartment lured me into thinking that we wouldn't accumulate much. The moving boxes laughed at me; I had been deceived.

We packed our one-bedroom Paris apartment almost as haphazardly as we packed up our Pittsburgh townhouse. It had equal excitement, even as we anxiously anticipated a move almost as foreign as our initial move to France. We were departing for another adventure that would take us far from the comforts of home.

The brown cardboard boxes that we placed into our coffee-n-cream SUV contained the memories of the life we rebuilt in Paris post-church. They contained the remnants of laughter and tears from a place that had been our sanctuary after we left the stone walls of the institution behind. It was a bit like our favorite game of Tetris, packing the boxes into our car.

We pieced life back together after the church much the same way we packed in those boxes – carefully, while turning each piece about, to ensure that it would fit with the foundation already laid. Time passed, our family changed, boys grew older, we prayed that we were growing wiser. Though home was changing again, the foundation of our family was much the same as it had always been.

Little Dragon was no longer squarely on my hip. He could carry me around now. Baby Chicken was as wild and feisty as ever, but he was also sensitive, gentle, and caring. My Valiant Knight remained by my side, this time driving our family to our newest iteration of home. It was always as it had been.

The same and yet… We had been through much.

Michelle Wahila

Somewhere between Paris moves (from the big apartment held together by a magnet and duct tape to our smaller one with far less duct tape), I realized how false my narrative had become. It was like emerging from a vivid dream; maybe, it was a nightmare. I woke up slowly. I was groggy.

I had been telling myself that I could not faithfully be pastor, wife, and mother. Once I let the darkness of that narrative creep in, it couldn't be stopped. Truth didn't exist outside of the institution. It was a downward spiral of lies that compounded. Eventually, that story corroded my self-confidence and self-worth just enough. It reminded me daily, hourly, and every minute that I wasn't adequate.

Some said that I put my family out as an idol ahead of me; I chose them over choosing to serve God where I had been called. Thank you, Jesus, for never allowing that lie to creep into my heart. They didn't need to be villains too. I stole enough from my loved ones; it broke my heart to be the thief.

My family existed together, but very far apart for those years. I pressed down so hard into the work that was cracking my heart, that it left only broken pieces of me to share. There was just existence.

When my #dreamlife crumbled, my family and the few I called friends helped me pick up the pieces. They told me the story that love is greater than failure. They hugged me as I reemerged from the darkness a different human than I was before *that* place. With open arms, they called me home.

The sound of the cuckoo song faded, and we began to hear the nighttime ribbiting of pond frogs. The glowworms greeted us; it was time to move from the comfort of our chairs. All four of us paused to take a final glimpse at the sunset that turned daytime to dusk.

Light met dark; I wondered if that was how it had always been. I had been too busy or too groggy to notice. Intermingled in the sky was a story of day meeting night, and the present looking ahead to the future. It is the vibrant place where the dark depths of sorrow meet the light of joy in hope.

Night met day in NY, Pittsburgh, Paris, and in the orchard behind a French farmhouse in the countryside. The pinkish orange crepuscule began to turn violet. Darkness crept in... Today's story – whatever it was – was finished. It was time to go home.

Michelle Wahila

A Blessing of Rosemary

Rosemary is one of the only edible things on the farm that stays through every season. Even the fact that it dries/preserves, is a testament to the way it remains. This herb for all seasons is the perfect reminder of the presence of the Divine with you in every season, particularly your harshest winters.

If you can find a bit of fresh Rosemary, you can bundle and dry it to use in cooking or to give scent to a room/closet/drawer.

Rosemary bundles, hope for the next season. Summer leads to Fall. Fall ushers in the darkness of Winter, but Winter whispers us into the newness of Spring and Spring brings us to Summer once again.

Hold a bit of rosemary in your hands as you offer this prayer:

Creator of all that is,
We hold in our hands a reminder of your plenitude –
Potent herbs
Whose essence enhances culinary wonders;
Whose sweet scent
Brings clarity and calm;
And who remain evergreen,
As signs of Your provision and protection.
Give to us the persistence of rosemary
That we might persevere
Until the day
We are called home
To be held in your hands.

High Pickle Season

I'M NOT SURE WHO THOUGHT IT WAS A GOOD IDEA FOR WEDDING SEASON TO overlap with gardening season; maybe it was the flowers. At any rate, this is where my two worlds collide, and where June gets particularly interesting. Life is never dull in June.

The first season in our new farmhouse was the perfect mix of leisurely chaos. We enjoyed the quiet of the countryside, learning new routines and enjoying long summer days outdoors. We immersed ourselves in the new rhythms that came with caring for a property so immense. In between, I learned the train route to and from Paris.

Betwixt trips to Paris, I took my gloved hands to the garden, carrying the spade and scuffle hoe to keep me company. When I stepped into the garden, I was surrounded with new life. There were shades of peach and violet, popping up where I didn't think flowers could grow. Abundant roses guarded our house, and carrots that we hadn't planted began to wave hello from the *potager*. The fullness of abundance enveloped me; I remembered what plenty felt like.

Amidst the pull of back-and-forth train rides, and vegetables that needed tending, I was learning to live within the newness of this life we had chosen. Transition came as often as the seasons; there was always something new to be done and new French vocabulary to learn in order to live.

It was this immigrant life pushing us further. This time, we were sojourners in the *campagne* (countryside). We had never ordered four cords of wood in Paris. There was plenty of new that necessitated growth. There were other things within us that were resuscitated.

———————

Though I had forgotten how to pray in Paris, in the country I was down on my knees every day. In the dirt, I planted and prayed. But mostly, I found a profundity of wisdom in the dirt of the countryside. It wasn't only in the new vocabulary, but it existed in the pace and shape of life. It was built into the transitions of seasons, and the days of the week.

The whirring of the tractors on Sundays were softer but as profound as the Sunday church bells. The farming life is one of cycles – toil and rest, harvest and sowing seeds in hope of harvest. The tractors murmured in the background of Sundays, stirring the quiet of the countryside into perpetual motion.

The motion of rural life was never as frantic as that of Paris, but it was not less ample either. It was easier to rise with the sun, greeted by rosy skies that appeared broader than the skies blocked by Haussmann buildings in the city. And though the city bustled toward sunset, in the countryside sunset came with a quieting of our labor and settling of our hearts. Dusk brought time to rest from the day's labor and a chance to toast to tomorrow's bounty in way largely absent in the dusk of the city.

The hope for what could spring forth tomorrow kept me expectant and grounded in today's dirt. My messy knees kept me humble; not everything planted would grow. Yet, the plants poking up from the dirt kept me honest – something would happen.

———————

Somehow it always happened in June, right in step with the profuse Paris wedding season. My life was the perpetual motion of back and forth, to and from places where I was meant to work and be. Sometimes I would arrive home from the city just in time to see the day's last light upon the garden. Even as the sun was setting, I could spot the new things that sprouted while I was away.

"I have my work cut out for me tomorrow." It was a matter of fact. You can't neglect the garden in June.

With the light of dawn, I whisked my dusty-pink gloves and clippers from their repose and tiptoed into the day's work. It wasn't a gesture of insecure slinking, but a desire not to disturb the progress of the flora I was stewarding. I was but an encourager of the vibrant green encompassing my life.

In my absence, the tomatoes intertwined themselves with the zucchinis, squishing the squash from their place. I tidied the vines, scolding them gently for stealing home away from the *courgettes.* "Everyone has a place here, my dears."

If I didn't spend so much time amidst the bustle of people during the height of June's wedding season, my family would have worried about my verbal encouragement of the vegetables. But I found comfort in cheerful song hummed for the creation. No masterpiece is made without encouragement.

Once the pumpkins were tamed, I dealt with the peppers. The spicy and sweet little horns were growing too fast to stand tall. I gave them the support of garden stakes and turned my eyes toward the knotted square that was the cucumbers.

The cukes were a mess, which was an unreasonable tale. I had only been gone for a day. June has a way of making potential reality. And my reality was a knotted mess of leaves.

The only way to deal with this mess was on my knees. I had heard that advice before. I took my foam garden kneeler and placed it at edge of the altar of cucumbers.

I plunged my hands into the cluster of vines. They clutched one another with their tendrils; maybe they clung to each other to grow. The unlatching of tendrils revealed the real story – cucumbers rested below.

Their knotted green blanket kept them safe from what was above. As I lifted the leaves, I spied more and more. It was a glorious hidden cucumber community, that had grown quietly underneath.

Prickly and poised, they were ready to go. I began plucking them up from their leafy hidden sanctuary. It was time to make room for more. The cucumbers of June crowd one another, begging to be sprung from their rest.

Every leaf lifted revealed another *cornichon*. Some were small and needed more time, but others had clearly been hiding in the thick of comfortable green. They grew overnight, I was certain!

"Where did you come from?" He had not been there two days ago. It was a mystery of June's magnificence.

My basket of cukes overflowed. Now the question became, "What do I do with abundance?"; had I asked that question before?

Even a Baby Chicken hitting his teenage growth spurt couldn't eat enough cukes to keep them at bay. It was the dilemma of June's abundant cucumber chaos. I was in a pickle.

My conundrum was also my answer, the pickle had to be pickled. I harvested and in between my Valiant Knight's own summer house tasks (mowing, chopping, and mulching), he would pickle. With the garlic preserved from spring's harvest and dill plucked with care from the summer herb garden, the pickling commenced.

The garlicky sour scent filled our kitchen with a story of abundance saved for later. My spouse would line up the jars, counting them off, calculating how long the pickles would last into winter. Unlike his pristine engineering equations, the pickle count was more fluid.

You could never count on the jars that would be consumed in one sitting by ravenous teens. I would wash the empty jars as rapidly as my Valiant Knight of Pickles could fill them. And our boys would enjoy sweet and sour pickled joy.

Once the boys were content, we counted again. Winter would enjoy pickles too. There was enough for joy to last into spring; I was certain that I once had heard that story too. We bottled and preserved joy for tomorrow, a gift from the lavishness of today. It was high season for abundance and pickles.

Michelle Wahila

A Planting Prayer

Though I do not know what tomorrow will bring, I will plant today in hope. I will ground myself in the messy labor of life with love. I will take up tools of peace, and sow joy into existence. Through the tempests, I will remain unwavering, committed to brave existence in a muddled world. I will toil for today, that tomorrow might come with abundance.

A Sparkly Pen and Chocolate Chip Cookies

THE SUNRISE OVER LA FAUVELIÈRE WAS BUBBLING UP IN HUES OF COTTON candy and creamsicle. The shades of my post-institutional church life were literally colorful, but it was also breathtakingly vibrant. From the bulbs who pop up in spring's first moments to the holly trees that adorn our winding sidewalks in winter, every season and cycle brought gifts from above. We painted ourselves into the vibrant landscape of this place, as if we had always been rooted here.

Every sunrise reminds us of the opportunity we have been given in living in this little oasis. Being on the farm has rooted us in time and space, quite literally in dirt, but also in reimagining what our lives might look like as immigrants in a foreign land. If only for a moment, our family belongs here.

We are known as the "American family," which in past times might have bothered me. I've come to embrace it boldly. Yes, I am the mom who shows up at the school gate at the end of the day with a Tupperware full of chocolate chip cookies to hand out. I'm the one wearing my very un-French hot pink sneakers and denim jacket straight out of the 1980s. I am here to show up as me.

I let my kids and all their friends laugh at my poor accent, but I muddle on anyways. And I embarrass the kids with the homemade

215

jam and flower bouquets that I insist their teachers, and their friends' parents, will love. Anyone who comes to our house in the summer is obligated to leave with a head of lettuce and at least one zucchini – sorry, those are the rules.

Woven gently into the landscape of farm life is the other part of my life – a train commute to Paris. Even though it is always bustling, it has become a quiet space that carries me to and from two places that each hold a piece of my heart. I both go home and come home with the calming rumble of the TGV train.

I live the most wonderful moments of life in the city, even if I no longer rest my head there at night. Sometimes I get to linger after my wedding and enjoy her glamorous buzz. I have coffee at the café and watch the people go by… The tourists and locals intermingled.

I pull a pink sparkly pen from the heart of my leopard bag. Once the rolling instrument that grounded me through meetings, she has a much lighter existence now. Next, a stack of cards comes up from the depths of my bag. A photo of the Eiffel Tower and small hearts grace the front of the cards: a rendering of the tower I was looking at from the café.

I sign my name with sparkles and swirls. My name was there to remind me who I was – "Love, Michelle" I wrote in all the cards. This was my signature and my heart's song. For all the moments I spent rolling that pen, wondering who I had become, I knew now. Signed for all to see, with love.

For so long, I had been focused on the future – of getting out, alive. Alive means different things, though. Alive means breathing physically but it also means being who you were created to be. By the time I left, I settled for the shallow breaths of marginally alive.

I had long ago felt the creativity and all the "me" seep out. To self-preserve I fixed my eyes on getting out alive. That was enough for this feminist misfit, ill-placed in a boardroom-shaped church, that was choking the creativity out my soul day by day. My only ambition was to get out with a me who was still me at all.

To protect what little I had left of myself, I fenced off my heart from Executive Jesus and told myself not to give him an ounce more of me than I had already offered. This meant gliding into the office exactly on time – not a minute before I needed to be there and not a minute late. I never wanted to be late so that the people around the table had extra excuses to grumble.

I was there when I needed to be. I would creep in almost unnoticed and bow to the cultural expectations of the morning exchange. I sat in my not-quite-assigned-but-definitely-not-at-the- head-of-the-table seat, unloading the necessities from my enormous bag packed for a day that wouldn't end until I turned into a pumpkin.

I decided I wouldn't speak unless spoken to – just like a good woman should. I wasn't interested in frivolous exchange or trying to dream with non-dreamers. I was interested in plain and simple survival. Self-preservation mode was difficult to maintain because it was the antithesis of how I desired to function in ministry.

I longed for a collegial connection beyond pleasantries. I settled for pleasantries. I sat quietly, armed with an army of gummy bears in my enormous bag reminding me that I deserved to sit at that table.

I was alive and present. I was seated at the table determined to claim my space, or at least to take up space. I took to rolling my pink-glitter pen back and forth on the big boardroom table to remind me that I was alive. It kept me from shrinking away entirely.

When the future finally arrived, it didn't feel like there was much of me left. I kept a few things to remind me of the time before. On the inside of my closet hung a hot pink sticky note with the word "joy" scribbled over it. I still had a glitter pen stashed in my enormous bag. From time to time, I would take it out and roll it over our dining table. Against the hard table, I felt what was true: I survived.

All these pieces of me, past and present, are contained in my little earthen vessel (cracks and all). I might be tempted to speak only of how far I have come. I could tell a story of all the ways that I have regained my identity in the arms of the Spirit's embrace. That narrative would be lacking authenticity, and the bleak parts of my story. The migraines helped to humble me too.

I am exactly who I was before it all began, but Lord, have I changed. I am somehow more – basking in love and in the shadow of the Tower that welcomed me on my first day and welcomes me still. With every sunrise, I recommit to showing up – for my family and friends, and yes, even myself.

I have equally recommitted to doing ministry in the ways that feel authentic to me, alongside the Jesus who continues to beckon me toward wholeness. The same God who paints vibrancy into the sunrise, is the One who has created and placed me here. With every breath, I am aware of how the little Divine light inside of me has been rekindled in the most imaginative ways – for which I am immensely grateful.

I will continue to show up. But I am showing up as me. I will always be a bit of a rebel because though I care deeply, I have learned to care much less about the rules. If you see me in Paris, I will probably be wearing pink sneakers, sipping coffee at a café, and signing my name with a glitter pen. If you come to the farm, you'll find me on my knees in the dirt, but don't worry, there will be a champagne toast after the dirt.

I'm growing back into my voice that will speak the ways of love more deeply into the universe. With raspberries, roses, champagne, and a Tupperware full of chocolate chip cookies, I will look for the good, and offer it where I am able, while resting in my quirkiness knowing that it will make me too much for some and not enough for others. I will continue to breathe in the privilege of this wild and holy calling. And I will live. I am going to live into all of *this* abundance.

Blessing the Mess (Two Ways)

For when you need more words:

Bless my heaping mess –
My failures and frailties,
My quirks and quandaries,
And every winding path
That leads me back to You.

Bless my splintered heart –
My sorrows and suffering,
My aches and anguish,
And every crack
That opens wide enough to welcome You.

Bless my jaded soul –
My regret and remorse,
My worry and woe,
And every cascade of tears
That is hesitantly presented to You.

For when You bless this –
My mess
Of a demolished heart and wrecked soul –
I know that You
Bless all of Me.

For when You bless My mess –
This heaping mess:
Torn and tattered,
Wandering and wrecked –
I know all of this Me
Is found unabashedly unbroken
And blessed
In You.

Michelle Wahila

For when you need fewer words:
Contributed with love from my friend and fearless editor, Anna. She can take
even my wordiest thoughts and edit them to shine.

failure
regret
aches

demolished
a pile of rubble

Known.

cracks
worry

wandering
hesitant
jaded

frailties   Seen.

Held.

splintered
torn
wrecked
suffering

In You.

tears
quandaries
anguish

all my heaping mess

Blessed.

The Raspberries are Tender

WHEN THE HOT DAYS OF SUMMER ROLL AROUND AND PEAK WEDDING season aligns with fruit season, there's no shortage of work. Just like my people, raspberries have the audacity to require care every single day. You can't leave them unattended, wedding or not.

They ripen into magenta more quickly than Little Dragon can eat them off their branches. In between weddings, I find myself in a raspberry patch each morning. The toil of picking and pruning is limitless in June. Not to mention the *confiture* requirement afterwards.

My dusty pink gardening gloves used to match the ripe berries, but now they are dirty with signs of time and fruitful harvests. You can't wear gloves to pick the raspberries. Once they've ripened, if you try to pluck them off the thorny branches with gloves, you mush them into something unworthy of jam.

I slipped off one pink protector, not ready to commit to being scratched on both hands. Raspberry thorns are wicked. They take in your clothes and leave you with one thousand and one small scratches before you realize what has happened. I didn't want one thousand and one wicked scratches again.

I wished I could shake the berries from their shrubby homes. My gloved hand was clumsy and bumbled about in the brambles. I frequently find myself a bit stuck among the berries when my gloves lead me astray. I tangled among thorns. The raspberries don't care if you're tangled. They require something much more tender than a gloved earthquake harvest.

My naked hand plucked the berries gently off their stems; there's no avoiding the thorns. I use my dusty pink gloved hand to hold down every branch. It does give some stability, but I must be vulnerable enough to reach out, in between the branches, without the safety of a glove.

I never thought I could take off the gloves. I had been fighting for far too long. The thought of being vulnerable sent my neck hairs to stand at attention. Putting myself in the position to be hurt was inconceivable.

The raspberries remind me that the risk of vulnerability is worth it, but it is tender work. It is also slow and a little bit tedious. But the reward is sweet.

I don't like tangling with the raspberries, but I do like jam. Once I accepted the gentle rhythm of plucking the magenta pink berries from among the thorns, I didn't resent the scratches nearly as much. I didn't like them, of course, but I stopped cursing them.

I learned how to use my clumsy gloved hand to clear the way before me of the worst thorns. My ungloved hand waited for its cue. It felt a little bare for such risky work, but I was ready to be gloveless in a world of sweet pink berries.

No one imagines themselves deep into adulthood caring simultaneously for teenagers and raspberries. They are both rather strenuous endeavors. Equally, you're not quite sure if you are going to get sour or sweet. But when they are sweet, they are oh, so sweet.

I saw the ways in which my Baby Chicken and Little Dragon had withstood the thousand and one thorny rough patches our family endured. I grieved the moments I lost to the late meetings. I regretted the memories absent thanks to my trauma-brain.

It was enough to make anyone want to retreat to the sanctuary of farm life and never re-enter society. If I thought about this possibility for more than a millisecond, I was sure that this would become my adulting plan. I scolded the thought from my head. Rather than daydreaming of a ridiculous fairytale future, I compelled myself to breathe in the very present farm-fresh air.

I made a rather fruitless attempt to capture the instant as a memory. I am so forgetful now; my brain hasn't been as resilient as my heart. It may not become a memory, but at least I had this flash of joy.

The little one was picking alongside of me, while the big one mowed perfectly straight lines, up and down the side yard. His baby chicken hair danced back and forth in the warm June breeze. Time hadn't stolen his fluffy strawberry cow lick from me.

It was comforting to look up and see the boys nearby, happily occupied by their rural country lives. It struck me how grown-up they were. Diaper days traded long ago for extreme sports and video games with a smattering of quiet farm life. I watched Little Dragon intently plucking raspberries from the bushes with the right amount of gentleness.

He picked faster than I did. Either unbothered by the thorns or a more skillful picker, he slid his ungloved hand in and out of the bramble bushes effortlessly. This is how it should be.

There was just enough bravery to tackle the thorns and resilience enough to plunge back into the bushes with the ease of a machine. His steadiness was breathtaking. I inhaled the slight scent of manure and exhaled proud momma.

Little Dragon was popping the spherical berries directly into his mouth, catching them between his rosy-pink lips. It was a beautiful cycle to observe. Engrossed in his mechanical but delicate movements, I was caught off guard by the tears beginning to well inside of me. I had missed so much of his little life.

Michelle Wahila

He was moving efficiently through the bushes. With all his swift-ness, his hand bumped mine. The soft warmth of his teenager-sized hand jostled me from my wandering thoughts back to the present. This was real. It wasn't a saccharine sweet, idealized dream of what life should be. This was the blessedness of everyday life, the kind that requires brave and gentle movement through the thorns.

A Prayer for Gentleness in a Thorny World

Lord, give me the bravery to move gently through a thorny world. Grant me a tenderness that is unwavering when I am tussled, scratched, and jostled about. Even though the past has been sharp with me, allow me to open my heart to the risk of vulnerability. Let the "me" of the present have just enough resilience to breathe in hope, and exhale with the strength of kindheartedness. Amen.

Sitting Fireside

It was dusk and the chill of the evening air chased us back inside. We were greeted by the warm glow of the fireplace already illuminating the coming darkness. The hearth sits at the center of our farmhouse. Open on two sides, it heats the stone farmhouse from the center. The flames danced in orange and red, providing warmth and light to our home.

Above the hearth are family photos, taken long ago. They are images of distant memories, of laughter and smiles that happened a lifetime ago. Baby Chicken and Little Dragon smile down from the hearth with chubby baby faces that glow as much as the fireplace below.

"I loved those faces," I thought to myself, as much larger, lankier versions of the photographs joined me on our oversized grey sofa. They flanked me like small soldiers guarding their Momma; the tables seemed to have turned. They snuggled into the couch beside me, wrapping themselves in the fuzzy black blankets into which I had immersed myself moments before.

We watched the flames spit and flicker. The wind rushed through the chimney enough that we heard it vibrate. The flames were unbothered and danced on, in twirls of orange. Apart from the vibrating, it was quiet.

The quiet was momentary, disrupted by the clinking of wine glasses. My Valiant Knight arrived with a goblet of red wine for each of us. Accepting the cup, I swirled the glass goblet around, making its burgundy contents swish side to side. I raised the cup toward my face and inhaled the scent of red fruits and wood. It was rich and full.

"Santé!" my Knight proclaimed, and we clinked our glasses together before raising them to our lips. In harmony, we sipped. The depth of its taste was as lush and complete as its aroma. I held the cup in both hands, firmly, but with the proper reverence for a cup so beautiful and full.

My spouse had squeezed himself in between myself and Little Dragon, negotiating his move by promising to rub the little one's head. It didn't matter how tall they got; they still wanted the comfort of being rubbed at night. Little Dragon shuffled over and accepted the caress of his Father's rough hands as the reward for his effort in moving.

We were all enveloped by the fuzzy blankets, settling into night and rest. The four of us managed to squeeze ourselves onto two cushions the way we once squished ourselves onto the black loveseat in Paris. Even though we had plenty of space now, we often found ourselves like this. All four of us were now watching the glowing flames. The deep vibrating of the chimney continued though the rest of the house was still. Dusk had fallen into night, and the only light left was that of the fireplace.

I glanced upward toward the baby photos adorning our mantle. I resisted the urge to be discontent. Time marched on, practically without me. I rested in knowing that those two little faces were growing into happy and healthy young men – tucked gently in, beside their mom and dad. They rested beside us, and we them. It was as it should be.

Each of us had come from our own version of a hard day – my spouse from his work, the boys from school, and me from a long day of travel. We had gone our own ways to work, live and play. But at the end of the day, we found our way back to each other and the grey sofa in the farmhouse that we called home.

We had made it home again. From the chubby-faced smiles on our family photos until that moment of fuzzy blanket rest, nothing was wasted. Happiness and distress in our work and all of our comings and goings intermingled to create even that moment in our story. I rested in that.

———————

Rest comes easier these days. From dusk until dawn, I give thanks that my once frenzied spirit finds quiet, and that sleep comes. The nightmares have lessened, and I am able to breathe again.

Though nothing has been normal in the path that led us here, there is a sacred normalcy in our lives now. It is a different, quieter rhythm than what once was. In the cozy couch moments, where three humans I love are snuggled in closely, I hope that we will always manage to find our way back together. After all, we have found our way thus far.

The fire's flames might briefly take me back to the rage that once burned inside of me, but it also dances away, into the past. It came and went without making my heart sink. I am neither burdened nor controlled by the past's stories, even those over which I had no control.

Instead, I offer them to the flames: the past as an offering of both grief and breath. The mix of sorrow and life that the Divine holds tenderly in her heart. It is that mix that makes me human and makes me, *me*.

On the path of authentic living, we must sojourn in both pain and joy. As we journey, we find ourselves becoming something new – something more. This, I am convinced, is the wholeness to which Jesus is continually calling us. This is the heart of Jesus I know and remember.

———————

My Valiant Knight untangled himself from the cozy wrap of blanket and people to place another log onto the fire. There were sparks. The piece of old oak crackled, and the once dampened flames came alive again.

It's breathtaking to see the spark that brings flame back to life. Our fire was aglow again. The fireplace is efficient, and the log is consumed, lighting the dark living room. As the flames rose, warmth radiated from the hearth, and we snuggled back into our places.

In my contentedness, I could not help but reminisce about all that had brought us to this moment. The intensity of both pain and pleasure that disoriented, disrupted, and reminded us of our humanity. The cycles and systems that entombed us. The choices – good and bad – that we made. "This is life, our life," I thought.

In much the same way, I contemplated how the trees from our forest bring warmth through the hearth in the center of our home during winter. The ash from the fireplace gives nutrients to our roses in the spring. The pastel roses adorn our home with joy throughout summer and well into fall. And when autumn arrives, the wood is split, hauled, and stacked in preparation for the cycle to begin again.

Nothing is wasted here. In every season, there is a place for everything – the ashes and the growth. Even that which is thrown into the fire brings the warmth of light through the darkness of night.

A Fireside Blessing

May this fire warm not just your hands, but your heart.
May its glow wrap around you like a familiar embrace.
May the crackle and pop of the flames remind you –
Life, in all its unpredictability, is full of surprises and sparks,
Even when we least expect it, even when we're a little singed.
May we welcome both the splendor and the soot of being human.

The Fuzzy Angel

LIFE IS ALWAYS FULL IN A FAMILY WITH TWO WORKING PARENTS AND TWO children. I imagined life becoming calmer as my children grew. In some ways this has been true. In other ways, phew. Parenting teens is not for the faint of heart.

It's not diapers and tantrums, but it's studying, exams, hormones, dating, and learning to navigate the harsh realities of life. It's a privilege to parent Baby Chicken and Little Dragon. They also have a way of keeping me on my toes. And Lord, I am a middle-aged lady going through changes of her own!

This kind of "full" requires every ounce of patience I can muster, and the fortitude to wade through studying thirteenth century agricultural France (more than once). The best weapon in the epic battle of studying is always laughter and 1980's music – definitely 80's music. The kids seem to think I am strange, but I lean into that.

I still spic-n-span the house on Fridays and I attempt to keep the farm dirt at bay the other days. I never expected teenagers to produce so much laundry, and the cooking? It doesn't matter how much I make; they eat it all and then wonder where the pizza is hiding. To be fair, my Valiant Knight also asks for pizza post-dinner.

You can imagine that I wouldn't want to take on more, in a pleas-

233

antly full life that has me caring for a farm and young men in between traveling for weddings. Then again, my Valiant Knight and I have always lived into adventure that has the potential to bring abundance. We're strange like that too.

Little Dragon began to ask for a dog since the moment he could say the word. In his toddler years he would ask and then tell me that he would, "Super wuv it, aww day yong." I am sure I would super love it all day long too, but there was no way a dog was fitting into church life or our tiny Paris apartment life, especially with two cats, a drum set, and several guitars already occupying space in our lives.

As Little Dragon grew into being able to write the word "dog," instead of simply speaking it, "dog" became central to every Christmas list, birthday wish, and an occasional "off the cuff" ask. He was nothing if not persistent. I had years of Christmas lists with DOG in the number one spot, serving both as a reminder of this precious "need" and a witness to the evolution of his perfect French handwriting.

Appreciating his perseverance, I began to crumble over the years. So, I started nudging my dearest spouse (who not growing up with animals has learned to love the kitten-beasts who have, according to him, invaded our home). Lucky for me, his exterior appears tough, but he is a softy at heart.

"But we have the space now!" was a valid argument from the Little Dragon, and how could we resist? It was serendipitous when I met the puppy lady at one of my weddings. She didn't just have puppies, she had *the* puppy.

The puppy had to fit farm life – caring for goats, happy to be outside, and still want cuddles. I'm the cuddle factor in the equation. If I was going to invest in training and caring for a puppy, there would need to be cuddles. It's a simple cost-benefit analysis.

And cuddles there are – ninety-five plus pounds of them. The fluffy baby is going to be enormous when he finally stops growing (much like my teenagers), and I'm certain we've invested in a polar bear not a dog. He is full of happiness and slobber and makes the dinner preparation entertaining because he noses my elbow ensuring I pay the cheese tax.

He brings an infinite amount of love and so much more mud into our home. I thought I swept up constantly *before* this new addition. For as much as I detested a wet-dog scented office, I now bear the scent of slightly wet dog as my perfume of choice.

But there's nothing like watching him sit by the big wooden farm gate waiting for his boys to arrive home, or seeing teenage boys run through the grass with an enormous furry creature chasing them. I also didn't expect Baby Chicken and Little Dragon to get down on the ground to cuddle him, but it warms my heart in every way. We do, in fact, love him all day long.

There's something to be said for risking love and leaping into adventure. It's not to be taken lightly; guarding the heart is paramount. We think, pray, and discern the Spirit's nudge, over and over again throughout our days on this earth. And we hope we choose paths that are both wise and faithful.

Sometimes we must correct paths that felt right but were not paths that led us to abundance. Other times, the rocky path is the only one ahead. We must tiptoe our way through terrain jagged enough to leave scars. Those passages penetrate and provoke.

Change so often comes with pain. Transitions of every sort stretch us beyond our capacity. We are pulled and prodded in directions we would not choose, and some of them we have chosen pain us still.

If we do find ourselves with scars of passage, we must admit that we have changed. We are so reticent to change, and yet the Spirit calls us toward transformation. As we have been created with love and Divine spark, we are called to re-creation and to creative existence that will bring love and light into the world. And Jesus, He is there too, beckoning us toward wholeness.

Transformation, re-creation, and wholeness, they are all ways to say what we don't love to do: change. When we lead already full lives, change brings disruption that most of us could do without, whether we are up for an adventure or not.

———

Change has a way of reminding us that our stories aren't yet finished. Our stories never exist separately from the continuous reshaping of the pieces of our lives that make us who we are – the work we do, our parenting, our passions, our singleness, our partnerships, and friendships.

There's love and risk in living into all the parts of ourselves that weave our stories together and into the universe.

We must be vulnerable when we screw up. And we must be brave enough to try again. It's risky business to be ourselves in the world. Yet, those unique pieces of who we are, become the foundation of curating a life that is whole because they contain the whole of who we are – stories of love and pain.

———

Packing up our lives to go from Pittsburgh, to Paris, to the countryside of France may seem a strange way to do life. It certainly has taken us on paths we would not have anticipated. They have also not been free of failure or pain.

At times it has been hard to admit to ourselves that there was pain along paths that seemed right and true. Though we might be tempted to say we chose unwisely, that doesn't fairly reflect our present nor the abundance we experienced along the way.

We have taken the risks of friendship, entrepreneurship, new jobs, new schools – of new life. There has been love in our steps. Equally, love has been set before us along the way. And you can't argue with love that has found you.

Love has found us all day long.

———

I also didn't expect to find love mixed with slobber, but a fuzzy angel lives with me now. On the hardest days, he motivates me to take the walk I probably need and breathe in the fresh air that fills my lungs with life. He's quick to sense pain and will stay by my side on the days when gardening and walking are difficult. He is a companion when the house is too quiet and an alarm clock throughout the day, reminding me to recommit myself to breath, or at the very least, to stop whatever I am doing and take him for a wee (also, no one wants to yell "potty" outside their door, so we refer to his outdoor deeds as "magic").

When the deepest scars seem to want to bleed again and the ache is too much to bear, I lie down next to this furry being who depends on me. He pulls me into the present with slobbery kisses or an enormous white paw to the face. When I call his name, and he comes running, I am reminded what love looks like.

Though I scold him when he munches on my rose bushes, he has settled into the farm life too. I wonder how I could be so lucky. Our home is filled with fur and joy, and our family feels more whole than it has in a long while.

Michelle Wahila

A Blessing for My Dog

May your life be full of adventure,
Your days bright with sun.
May you find comfort in my arms,
Warmth at my feet,
And peace at my side.

For the Love of September

SEPTEMBER WAS ALWAYS MY FAVORITE MONTH IN PARIS. THE CITY QUIETED from summer's tourists and the normal rhythm of life resumed with school, commuting, and weddings. It was still warm enough to forego the Parisian scarf, and the sky blue enough to be picture perfect. September was the delightful threshold between summer skies and winter's darkness in the city.

To every couple excitedly choosing their wedding date, I suggested September. With a sunrise less ridiculous than June, and a chance of precipitation so low it would make November blush, September was the perfect month to marry in the City of Light. It would bring joy to my heart when a couple's survey came back to me with September in its heading. It's easy to prepare for perfect.

Preparation is everything when it comes to Paris wedding days because Paris likes to be unpredictable enough to maintain her mystery. It means that no matter how well you plan or how detailed your wedding day schedule looks, the most romantic city in the world might have other plans for you on your wedding day.

It could be strikes (this is the French way), a movie being filmed, or a foot race set up around your chosen wedding location. For foot races I am prepared with my chrome Nikes and I am not afraid to cross the line and run with the clinking of champagne glasses cheering me onward. Not every hiccup can be foreseen, but even in September's perfection, we pray that Paris will be gentle with us on wedding days.

―――――――

I called the museum to ask permission to perform a small ceremony on a staircase. Even the staircases of Paris are mesmerizingly beautiful, and you wouldn't want to stand there upon them without the nod of the city herself. I had done my due diligence.

We arrived before sunrise, as we always do. For the prettiest pictures we begin before the city begins to come to life. Wedding days greet the sunrise with promises of love. If only all days could begin the same way.

I arrived at the staircase with the grooms' family and friends – dressed to the nines and in awe of the golden gates that elegantly gave the most magnificent backdrop to our staircase. "Iconic!" someone whispered under her breath.

I fluffed dresses, fixed fascinators, and straightened one or two ties. We were prim and proper and ready to begin, just as the sun started to peek over the horizon. But before any perfect beginning comes a prologue filled with strife; in this case, a fluorescent orange armband with the word "*sécurité*" written around it.

In flowing French that rolled off his tongue, he told me that we could not stand there. But stand there we must – so in my less than flowing *français* I begged for twenty minutes of time. As I negotiated with the staircase statute enforcer, I reached into my pocket for the tiny piece of white plastic resting inside.

I slipped it inside of my lace collar and claimed my role as pastor. The *Monsieur* of the *Escalier* had wider eyes and softer words that matched well the timing of the rectangle's introduction to my collar. "But it's a day for love," I hummed with a soft voice and smile.

Maybe he had never seen a pastor in lipstick or maybe his heart was won with love. For the next half an hour he promised us the stairs for our wedding in this city of love. A small crowd gathered to stand on the stairs alongside of the security guard who now shielded us. *"Chut! Chuuuut!"* he hissed toward bystanders.

The shushed crowd stood in dutiful silence. Then the cape-clad second groom arrived to his September wedding day. The hush was replaced with a "Gasp!" No words could have been spoken to capture it better.

The September breeze was on cue, lifting the cape that swirled behind him in a dance. Florals in hues of magenta, sherbet orange, and sunny yellow adorned the shoulders of the dancing cape. I caught a glimpse of a monarch settled into his shoulder, placed with care by the artist of the cape.

A portrait of love, set against golden gates, with security who broke all the rules. The crowd clapped and we cried all together. Love was dressed in a cape and tuxedo that day.

We toasted and cheered, and "Congratulations!" rang aloud. I gave thanks to the man who said rules didn't matter for a half an hour at sunrise in Paris. We bid our new friends farewell, and the two very married grooms held hands to descend the stairs. The cape waved a silky goodbye as epic as her entrance. Another perfect September day…

It was me, the rogue pastor, who stood on those stairs, asking for the rules to be bent. I gave up on Executive Jesus's perfection so long ago, so I was brave enough to ask. My focus and work turned toward love, away from the politics and patriarchy that kept me trapped in rules of the past. I threw in the towel on church and came out with a heart full of joy.

My hope is that what I learned in my last season will somehow carry over into the next one. I am also kind of hoping that even if I am not running with arms wide open into the next season, that I won't resist it. It will take love-soaked courage, I am confident of that.

I didn't really "leave" church, but I see the work of church as more creative and less traditional. Blessing belongs to all of us – whether it is inside or outside of the church doors. Every couple, every person, that seeks this kind of soul-touching moment deserves to receive it.

We don't have to try very hard to see where the church has failed love. Human hypocrisy overshadows Divine love too often. We shouldn't be surprised that people are bored or fed up with traditional religion. Institutional scars have a far reach and a breadth that should bring lament to our lips.

I have the privilege of standing outside the church doors, wearing my lace-sleeved clergy dress and collar. Though I lost that piece of me for a moment, love encouraged me to slide that piece of plastic back into my collar and blessing back into my life.

I get to marry *all* the couples. The only requirement is a desire for love and blessing.

They don't have to look a certain way or dress a certain way. They need not be "religious" at all. They can be 100% who they are, and I get to tell that story. In my tradition, *love* walked among us – He showed us the way. We get to follow along.

I was finally eager to get back to work; I didn't have a ticket to punch this time. I'm not sure that I have found love-soaked courage yet, but I continue that journey and pray. I am gentler and braver than I once was, and I am certain that whatever comes next, there will be hands to hold along the way.

It was the end of the September cape-clad wedding day – a perfect day by all accounts. I was tucking my Baby Chicken into his bed. I thought back to an evening, long before his growth spurt and teenagerdom, when we shared our day while cuddling under a fuzzy dinosaur blanket.

"Did you marry people well today?"

"I hope so! What do you think?"

"Did they laugh?"

"They most certainly did; we all laughed." We giggled as I squeezed his little hand in mine.

"Did they cry?"

"Yup, they cried too."

"But is that love?" He asked me so sincerely with wonder in his eyes.

"Yes, love is both," I whispered his way. His eyes widened.

"Then how do you know it is real?"

"Because love makes you more *you*."

Without skipping a beat, and still holding my hand, he looked up at me with his one-sided grin, "Mom, why are you so small?"

"Because God made me this way."

"Mom, you're beautiful."

I am the tiny keeper of small things in Paris – tissues and veils, champagne and roses – I hold them all in their places until it is time to tell the world a love story, one couple at a time. Is it beautiful? I hope so. I'm starting to believe so myself. Sometimes it takes a little hand holding and a little rage to remind us of our own irreplaceable beauty.

Michelle Wahila

Old, New, Borrowed, Blue Blessing

We give thanks for something old, and the way this token anchors us to the past. With gratitude, we present something new, offering it in hope for the future. We accept something borrowed as a gift of community surrounding us in this moment. We hold in our hands the wonder of something blue, a symbol of faithfulness and love into eternity. May these treasures, marked with love, bear witness to the sacred moment before us and the partnership being created this day. Amen.

Successful Misfit

ONE OF THE UNINTENDED CONSEQUENCES OF STEPPING AWAY FROM A traditional ministry inside the church doors, into a creative endeavor outside the church doors, is that I have become a rather successful misfit. I prefer it that way. I'd rather be drawn into the embrace of the wonderers and wanderers than the noted and notorious.

Today, the most unexpected dings in my inbox don't come from those serving Executive Jesus, but the ones trying to hold onto any notion of Jesus at all. As I began to tell my story in bits and pieces, other pastors flooded my inbox. And I began to hold the stories of others, as well as make space for their tears.

It was not a ministry in which I ever wanted to partake, but it is necessary and sacred all the same. There have been too many casualties of a broken system, and people are worth more than an existence of living as collateral damage at the feet of Executive Jesus. We must break the cycles of power and protection that allow for it, while clinging to a Jesus that will help heal the wounds of those left behind.

Presbyterians are supposed to have the ability to dialogue and even dissent without breaking down into chaos. We hold the principle that "people of good faith may differ" near and dear to our Presbyterian hearts. While we may strive to do things "decently and in order," we believe that real discussion across the theological/political aisle doesn't break down faith but bolsters it.

Real, of course, is the key. If we aren't seeking to live an authentic existence with the people around us, we cannot have authentic conversations about the hard things; it's just not possible. Shying away protects the system but not the people within it.

This principle also allows for minds to be changed and for the continuation of the work of the Holy Spirit among us. At the intersection of hard conversations and the breath of the Holy Spirit, the church doesn't just move forward – she fulfills her purpose.

It takes all of us to be the Body of Christ, not just a select few seated at the table. It equally takes difficult conversations around the table to propel us forward. It is not an either/or, but a both/and kind of messy, difficult life together to move forward with any sort of concern for those who are living in the margins of church or society. Jesus cares about the people there; we ought to too.

Every individual institution that is a part of the bigger church is called to live out the Great Ends of the church.[1] They are lofty challenges; we don't take them lightly. It's necessary to continually discuss, refocus, and reevaluate vision to edge ever closer to fulfilling our purpose.

Sometimes when we neglect to have meaningful, albeit hard, discussions concerning our purpose and vision, we begin to look inward more than outward. This is not to say that we should not focus on our own individual spiritual walk, but it is to say that an insular focus can disrupt and distract from ministry. And it is when we are distracted that the system takes over – we go on autopilot and do things the way they have always been done.

---

1. The Great Ends of the Church are: the proclamation of the Gospel; the shelter, nurture, and spiritual fellowship of the children of God; the maintenance of divine worship; the preservation of truth; the promotion of social righteousness, the exhibition of the Kingdom of Heaven to the world. (PC (USA) Book of Order F-1.0304)

When we are satisfied with the way things have always been done, we will inevitably begin to rest rather than resist. The church has done its fair share of resting, and we can point to myriad examples of the way this complacency has caused harm. Every once in a while, though, the church gets it right and is able to transform a conversation about hard things into a way forward that draws people closer to Jesus.

When I was newly ordained, I sat through many a Presbytery meeting that debated the personhood of our LGBTQIA+ siblings. This was hardly a "people of good faith may differ" issue, though some saw it in that light. Others of us knew it was a much deeper issue of acknowledging the humanity of all of God's children.

Conversations surrounding right to marry and ordination sucked the air out of the room at almost every meeting. There were debates and discussions aplenty. I would glance over at my Gracious Mentor, and when it was time, we would stand to be counted.

We stood in the minority, until we didn't. The breath of change finally came. This might make it sound easy, but it wasn't. Churches left, administrative commissions were formed, ruling elders risked losing their ordination. It was a tumultuous and risky time in the church – it was also my welcome into the world of Presbyterian polity lived out in real time.

I watched the leaders within the Presbytery take courageous stands. I saw the differences between protest and power, and I also saw pleas of faith. At the time, I could not have envisioned a church that would issue an apology for the ways my LGBTQIA+ siblings were harmed by the system. Thanks to the faithful witness of many, we have a story that begins to speak of harm done in the name of Jesus and points us toward forging a new path ahead.

The road ahead, after harm has been done and recognized, is a circuitous path. It requires repentance and reparations. In a system as large as my own denomination, it also requires all local churches to not only adopt the polity but to embody policies that support it. It's an easier said than done scenario and it is only the smallest of steps toward a church that looks more like Jesus.

Today, however, I have married people who never believed they could have a pastor bless them and I have held The Cup in the most peculiar of places that didn't look like "church." These small things point me to the possibility of what church could be... I want to be caught up in a broader vision of such possibility. In taking on the role of pastor in a less traditional way, I hope that I might catch a glimpse of the Spirit in her creative work outside the church doors too.

The role of pastor never ceases to amaze me. I witness the greatest triumphs of love and the deepest heartbreaks. There is no greater privilege than accompanying people through it all. I see the tears, the laughter, and the love woven into people's stories.

Very rarely are stories all good or all bad; black or white. Theology and the work of ministry, therefore, becomes about thinking in the grey. It turns out that the longer I remain in ministry, the less I have come to understand black and white answers to theological questions, and the more I have become comfortable with hosting theological dialogue amidst the grey.

It is a reflection, I believe, of life. In the hard things, we are rarely faced with questions that have black and white answers. More often life's hardest choices have grey answers: multiple options, various outcomes, consequences, and effects on us.

The best theology addresses how we are to live faithfully and with grace amid the grey, and welcomes people into this nuanced and full space. How do we love people well through the hard-grey-decision-making processes? How do we love people through the various outcomes, options, and consequences? How do we see the Spirit working through the grey to create a more abundant and colorful world?

With the most unexpected dings of my inbox and the most glorious weddings, I witness miracles – stories of love and rebirth tucked into the grey. With every story, my own hopefulness is renewed. Because I have seen love-soaked courage in the world, I can hold hope for the same.

And I can begin to tell my own story too.

I am going to tell the story of who I am now, not simply who I was before. That too, is a privilege, because I get to point to the places where the Spirit continues to comfort and compel. She is working still. I will work too; with energy, intelligence, imagination, and love, I will press onward. It's not always a delightful task, but it is a vibrant and holy one.

Michelle Wahila

A Welcome Prayer

Welcome into this space of grace:
We open the doors, and with them, our hearts.
Blessed is the gathering of saints, both familiar and new.

May we laugh freely, share authentically, and listen kindly. Blessed is
the gathering that unfolds with love.

In the beauty of connection, may we find ourselves.
Blessed is the gathering that unfolds in curiosity.

For this moment of shared presence, we offer our gratitude. Welcome,
saints, into this space of grace:
Here's to the path that unfolds before us.

Epilogue

It is said that time has a way of healing all wounds. There is, of course, truth to that. Time also has a way of lending us space - a place in which we not only heal but are granted the grace to embody our stories in new ways.

This story has been told and retold and has gone through a multitude of iterations on the page. My earliest beta readers told me there was no hopeful arc in the story! I knew that hope must have the final word in my narrative, but I wasn't in the place at the time to see how.

Then a little thing called Covid came to be. Our world was thrust into something that most of us could never have anticipated, and what we knew as normal was no more.

For my family, Covid meant being confined to forty-two square meters except for the one precious time per day when we were afforded our "exercise." Day to day life shrank to fit within a one-kilometer radius from one tiny Parisian apartment.

Yet, our existence was full. We made homemade pizza for dinner and daily popcorn for afternoon movies. We played games and made music together. Each day after lunch, I delivered a sliver of chocolate to the three of my men, holding it as carefully as a communion wafer in worship. I made coffee to accompany the chocolate, and my spouse and I toasted to the comfort of chocolate in a time of unknowing.

I learned to play the bass to accompany my husband on his ukulele. Little Dragon could frequently be found banging away on the electric drums. We all belted it out in our forty-two square meters. I'm sure our neighbors loved us.

I was managing two grades of school for two boys while my dear spouse worked in the kids' shared bedroom. We zoomed and zoomed and cried a little too. Our living room - weight room - dining room housed school and family – night and day.

I saw a business that I had grown from nothing return to nothing. Weddings ceased; tourism stopped. We wondered if we would be able to leave France if something happened to our family stateside.

There was grief for the moments lost with friends and family. Holidays passed with the four of us hunkered down in our Paris apartment. There was also thankfulness for our family's health during this unprecedented time. And finally, there was deep joy found in seeing great advancements in medicine that would bring us vaccines.

To its very core, life changed. Like so many of life's transitions, it was neither completely good nor completely bad, but it was profound. It reprioritized much of our life together.

The reimagining of our life included a move to the countryside. It meant learning new commutes (and for my Valiant Knight learning to ride a motorcycle!), the anxiety of entering new schools, the loss of community, and the challenge of living a vastly different life than we had in Paris.

Oh! And running a farm.

I needed to make room for a new life without the pressure of telling a story about my old one. At times, I was tempted to drop the whole thing, the question "Why bother?" echoing into my very core.

After all, my motivation was not about revenge or even to seek accountability for harm. Further, I carry a deep love for many of the people still in the institution, trying to do the good Lord's work every day. I have a great deal of empathy for those caught up in the system, even those who you might be tempted to call bad actors. There's no villain in this story other than Executive Jesus and the system that both created and serves him.

When we muster the courage to tell our stories (even the hard parts) we begin to see all the places the Divine has been working in the nooks and crannies of our messy lives. This is, in essence, what the Biblical witness affirms.

God works in and through us. The stories of faith show us that in our messiness, and even to the depths of hell, God is moving. We trust in the truth of these stories, and alongside our own, we proclaim that love wins.

When we come to embody our story, we also come to embody the Divine more deeply. We are intertwined with the communion of saints in love, and we are called out into the world in, with, and through Divine Love. By our loving movement in the world, as messy as that might be, hope meets reality.

And when we are undone by a messy world, love has a way of picking up our broken pieces and refashioning us into something more. These are the places where we become more ourselves, and more like the loving God who is with us through it all. Not only is it "more," it is a miracle.

At its foundation, my story is one about healing and hope, because it is also a story about faith.

Telling my story is now a bit easier, thanks to the gift of time and space and of the stories shared with me by so many others. In writing and telling my story, I have had the privilege to sit with others telling theirs – many of whom have been deeply wounded by the institution of the church. Hearing their stories has given me courage to find my own voice again, even after putting this story away for so long.

This place, into which I have reemerged anew, is a healthier and happier place. I have the breadth and width to tell the hardest parts of my story with grace. I am both gentler and braver in my telling. This, in and of itself, is miraculous. Though I always knew time heals, I wasn't sure I would ever come into this space.

Epilogue

This space is also one that gives the story back to the Divine Source of Love. It is the reason these pages are filled with stories alongside of liturgies and blessings. It is in the prayers that I have truly found my voice. The words bring life to the places where the telling of my stories were void of it. They have become the hopeful arc once missing.

The words are for celebrations and the everyday. Written for times of both sorrow and joy, they are the pulse of this book. And they are, I think, what prayer is meant to be – filling the cracks and crevasses of our hearts, in the holy moments where the Divine meets us. Their purpose is to intertwine with breath and words, light and love, the Divine Story with our own.

Though ultimately stories may ruffle us, it is in our receiving and listening that we are transformed. And new life is all about transformation. The Divine Story of Love has shown us the way of abundant new life.

My only hope is that we can come to embrace this truth, not once or twice, but over and over again – until our stories are woven into eternity. The power of this kind of storytelling is a vibrant gift, given to a messy world. It reminds us that in our becoming is abundance.

Maybe the generations that come after us will even tell our stories, alongside of the stories of faith. Stories of the Divine, given in Divine Love to Divine Image Bearers. This is a gift, but most of all this is real, true, authentic love.

And my goodness, don't we need a little more love in the world?

A Morning Blessing for a New Day

I rise to greet this day. Lord, take the things of yesterday that still fill my mind – my fears, failings, and triumphs – and grant me the fortitude to live today anew. I am not separate from my history, but it does not define who I am today. Stir in me something fresh, that invites me to embrace the virtue of the present. Though I might fear today, be near. Though I might fail today, bring comfort. If I should triumph today, encourage me. Give my heart permission to delight in today.

www.ingramcontent.com/pod-product-compliance
Lightning Source LLC
Chambersburg PA
CBHW070918120626
46546CB00001B/309